In his extensive travels, Dave Breese comes in contact with many and varied Christian groups. What he has seen disturbs him.

"Many Christians appear to be dangerously vulnerable to cultic influences", he says.

What about you?

Are you vulnerable?

Do you know the marks of cults? Can you spot error even before it takes on all the aspects of a full-blown cult? This book can arm you against the father of lies. Satan will introduce error whenever and wherever he can. Don't be his victim.

Know the Marks of Cults!

About the Author

Dave Breese travels some 75,000 miles a year, much of it in preaching evangelistic crusades and in speaking to college students. He is a member of the Board of Administration of the National Association of Evangelicals and is well known in evangelical churches of various denominations.

He has written two previous books, *Discover Your Destiny* (Word) and *His Infernal Majesty* (Moody Press). He is heard frequently on the radio broadcast "Pause for Good News," a daily five-minute presentation carried on commercial stations and sponsored by "Back to the Bible Broadcast."

Breese makes his home in Hillsboro, Kansas, with his wife Carol and daughters Lynn and Noelle. He claims one famous relative, Samuel F. B. Morse, inventor of the wireless, whose third name was Breese.

Know The Marks of Cults

Dave Breese

This book is intended for the reader's individual use and profit. However, it is also designed for group study with the aid of a leader's guide, available from your local bookstore or from the publisher at 95¢.

VICTOR BOOKS

a division of SP Publications, Inc., Wheaton, Illinois

Offices also in Fullerton, California • Whitby, Ontario, Canada • London, England

Fifth printing, 1978

Library of Congress Catalog Card Number: 75:21907

ISBN: 0-88207-704-x

© 1975 by SP Publications Inc. World rights reserved
Printed in the United States of America

VICTOR BOOKS
A division of SP Publications, Inc.
P. O. Box 1825 • Wheaton, Ill. 60187

DEDICATION

To my daughter Lynn,
with love,
hope,
and prayer

CONTENTS

PREFACE

It all started at a wedding.

Knowing I would have to sit in silence for 10 or 20 minutes before the ceremony and an equal time after, I took with me a small pamphlet about one of the cults. I read the helpful pages with interest and profit. The reading of the pamphlet, however, reminded me that it would take a whole library of books to analyze in detail each of the strange religions attracting people in our time.

But what if one could present in simple, readable fashion the marks that characterize the entire gamut of individual cults? That could be eminently helpful!

That same evening I made notes of the general cult characteristics that I had observed. The result of those notes was a pamphlet entitled "The Marks of a Cult," which has been distributed by the tens of thousands across America and on many overseas mission fields.

The response from Christian leaders, pastors, radio broadcasters, and individual readers was most encouraging. Many requested additional material on the subject of the common religious heresies that are becoming fashionable today.

The editors of Victor Books indicated their interest in the expanded material very specifically. They requested a full manuscript on the subject, expressing the conviction that a study of these doctrinal principles would be helpful to churches, Sunday Schools, and Christians in general across the world. Their encouragement was decisive, and the results are before you in the following pages.

I wish to express my sincere thanks to faithful people who have rendered valuable aid. The first among these is Elmer Flaming, friend and father-in-law, who gave me the initial encouragement that it always takes to get a writing project underway.

I am grateful also to Jackie Maplesden for her tireless research of the Los Angeles press, to Luella Yoder for her patient compilation of the tiresome cult pronouncements, and to Ruth Friesen for research, compilation, and manuscript preparation, all efforts beyond the call of duty.

The ideas and thoughts in this manuscript were greatly influenced by conversations with faithful pastors, youth directors, and Christian workers with whom I have had the blessed opportunity to serve in the ministry of evangelism across the world. They are a noble group who are carrying on the battle for truth in the front lines of today's spiritual conflict. God bless them all.

The writer invites responsible correspondence by those who would present questions, suggestions, or further illustrations of the points contained herein. This material is presented with the hope and prayer that it will glorify our only Lord and Saviour, Jesus Christ, and advance His Gospel in these days in which truth is being challenged on every hand.

Dave Breese
Christian Destiny, Inc.

P. O. Box 100
Wheaton, Ill. 60187

INTRODUCTION

We are living in a day when many are attempting to move beyond Christianity.

Because of the myths of progress in vogue today, the word "beyond" has a certain appeal. Something that is forever fixed and changeless seems in the minds of some to be stodgy and undynamic. In this existential age, things must forever progress, engined by the dynamism of a newly discovered life-force in our time. The prevailing emotion of this civilization is not love or hate or anything so activistic; it is boredom. We demand new fascinations to feed our ever-shortening spans of interest.

This demand for new fascinations has led many to try to move beyond the faith once delivered to the saints to something newer (and therefore presumably truer) and more exciting. I will always be grateful for the words of Dr. Eastburg, my philosophy professor at Northern Seminary, who said, "If it's new, it isn't true; and if it's true, it isn't new."

Christianity should not be thought of as a stone wall behind which we cannot get. It is rather the highest mountaintop beyond which it is downhill no matter which way one goes. There is nothing greater, nothing higher, and certainly nothing more magnificent than the mountaintop of divine revelation in Scripture and in Jesus Christ. To move beyond that mountaintop in the pursuit of something better is to lose oneself in the crags and crevices of the slopes that fall away from real Christianity. And beyond the crevices of heresy are the fever swamps of the cults, where the serpents and the scorpions wait. Beyond rationality is insanity, beyond medicine is poison, beyond sex is perversion, beyond fascination is addiction, beyond love is lust, beyond reality is fantasy.

Just so, beyond Christianity is death, hopelessness, darkness, and heresy.

Nevertheless, people continue to be offered those side paths whose ultimate direction is downward. The increasingly complicated religious situation of our time is producing an explosion of the strangest religious concoctions ever brought to the mind of man.

This book is presented with the hope and prayer that it will be used to point up those errors most characteristic of the cults of our time. It is not really a study of the cults themselves; they are deserving of no such attention. It is rather an expression of hope that we may develop the spiritual facility to recognize instantly the marks of the cults. This will save us the bother and expense of further involvement.

We may also note that the same characteristics of religions that are out-and-out cults can have beginning tendencies within the true Church of Christ. The recognition of those characteristics which may be cultic, coupled with their early correction, may prevent future spiritual tragedy.

Writing to the Corinthians, the Apostle Paul suggested that they examine themselves to be sure that they are "in the faith" (2 Cor. 13:5). This admonition, coupled with the warning that in the

11

latter times some shall depart from the faith (1 Tim. 4:1), should be cause enough for each of us to make careful doctrinal examination of himself.

The clear teaching of Scripture is that if we would judge ourselves, we would not be judged by God (1 Cor. 11:31-32). When one corrects his course in time, he shortens the process of sometimes painful spiritual correction. The absence of doctrinal correction produces spiritual ruin. How many disillusioned Christians have stood amid the broken pieces of their shattered lives and said, "If only I had known. Why did not someone warn me in time?"

It is our prayer that these pages will bring a timely warning.

1 | Why Do Cults Prosper?

"I am the lord of the universe!"

These words were spoken by a young guru on a recent tour of the United States as he addressed 30,000 adoring devotees in Houston, Texas. On-lookers viewed with astonishment the spectacle of these young followers prostrating themselves in worship before their "perfect master."

Many people, knowing of such spectacles, ask new questions concerning the astonishing rise of strange religious leaders in our time. They see otherwise rational acquaintances of theirs give themselves to a new religious fanaticism, professing ecstatic conversion to the cause of some flaming messiah who has helped them discover a new and sacred truth.

It seems a mounting number of evangelical Christian congregations are increasingly concerned over the disappearance from their midst of whole families who have slipped away from the faith into an unheard-of religion. "What is going on in our time?" they ask. "What strange new cults are assaulting the minds of people?"

A cult is a religious perversion. It is a belief and practice in the world of religion which calls for devotion to a religious view or leader centered in false doctrine. It is an organized heresy.

A cult may take many forms but it is basically a religious movement which distorts or warps orthodox faith to the point where truth becomes perverted into a lie. A cult is impossible to define except against the absolute standard of the teaching of Holy Scripture. When contrasted to biblical truth, a cult is seen to have distinguishing marks by which it can be labeled as being fatally sub-Christian.

There is no question but that one of the most interesting and dangerous developments of our time is the rise of aberrative religions. The promoters of old and new cults are active, and their works are growing as never before. Emboldened by easy successes, they believe they can capture new multitudes of followers.

The result is that millions of simple souls are being beguiled into following religious notions that are nothing but false and satanic cults. The old cults are experiencing a remarkable resurgence, and curious new "faiths" are spawning in profusion.

When people hear of the strange beliefs and practices of the cults that share in today's religious resurgence, they understandably ask why. "Why are so many men, women, and especially young people attracted to those unorthodox spiritual leaders and their strange, suspicious practices?"

In answering that question, we must first of all remember that the Bible predicts that true Christianity will be under the constant attack of those who would deny and destroy the faith. One of the most moving speeches in the New Testament is the Apostle Paul's words of warning to the elders of the church at Ephesus when he bade them farewell and admonished them to take proper care of the church.

> "Take heed therefore unto yourselves, and to all the flock, over the which the Holy Ghost hath made you overseers, to feed the church of God, which He hath purchased with His own blood. For I know this, that after my departing shall grievous wolves enter in among you, not sparing the flock. Also of your own selves shall men arise, speaking perverse things, to draw away disciples after them. Therefore watch, and remember, that by the space of three years I ceased not to warn every one night and day with tears" (Acts 20:28-31).

Here Paul warned the Ephesian elders (and all subsequent Christians) that they would be subject to the attack of the enemy from two quarters, within and without. Grievous wolves would come in from the outside. Also, those who would seem to be members of the flock would "arise, speaking perverse things, to draw away disciples after them."

Because of this, the elders were told that they must "take heed, watch, and remember." They were never told that they should be merely popular leaders, fashioning a message which would promote consensus among various points of view. Rather, they were to be faithful custodians and teachers of the eternal, absolute truth of God.

This commission to the elders of the Early Church is surely the more valid for those who are custodians of the work of God in our particular time. There seems little question but that we are living in the day predicted by the Apostle Paul when he said, "Now the Spirit speaketh expressly, that in the latter times some shall depart from the faith, giving heed to seducing spirits, and doctrines of devils" (1 Tim. 4:1).

Why then are people attracted to false religious doctrines and practices as against true commitment to Jesus Christ and His Church? A number of reasons for this spiritual defection are given to us in the Word of God.

1. Love of Darkness

"And this is the condemnation, that light is come into the world, and men loved darkness rather than light, because their deeds were evil. For everyone that doeth evil hateth the light, neither cometh to the light, lest his deeds should be reproved. But he that doeth truth cometh to the light, that his deeds may be made manifest, that they are wrought in God" (John 3:19-21).

A person determined to live an immoral life, or even a self-centered one, will flee from the truth of the Gospel of Christ which shows up his life for what it is, an offense to God. One of the chief reasons people refuse to believe the true Gospel of Christ after they hear of the truth of God is its ruthless illumination of sin and its call to repentance and faith in the Saviour.

In this same vein, one of the primary reasons professing Christians defect from their allegiance to

Christ is that they have fallen into sin and refuse to return to fellowship with God on the basis of repentance and faith.

"He that doeth evil hates the light" and therefore will continue to walk in and love darkness. While walking in darkness the sinner imagines that his evil deeds are unknown to God and to his fellowmen. Nothing could be more foolish! No one can hide his thoughts or actions from the God who sees everything. "All things are naked and opened unto the eyes of Him with whom we have to do" (Heb. 4:13).

Despite this fact, there are those who foolishly go on refusing to recognize the moral law of God. They choose rather to embrace a false doctrine that excuses their immoral or self-centered lives. They foolishly prefer the ever diminishing pleasures of sin and selfwill to the joy of Christ's forgiveness and life.

Often this kind of person is attracted into a false religion. Though its requirements may be stringent, he can still retain his rebellion against God or independence of Him. He can still go his own way to some degree.

2. Spiritual Immaturity

The period in our Christian lives when we are most vulnerable to the subversion of false doctrine is when we are in our spiritual infancy. When we step out of darkness into the light of the Gospel, believing in Jesus Christ, we are justified by faith. At this point we become what the Scripture calls "a newborn babe" (1 Peter 2:2). Few eras in our Christian lives will be more fresh, beautiful, and thoroughly enjoyable. Our testimonies will probably reveal the ecstasies that are now ours in knowing Jesus Christ.

Many a Christian hymn writer has expressed the fresh, beautiful delight of the heart that has discovered the reality of salvation in Christ. Everything is different, as Robinson suggests,

> "Heav'n above is softer blue,
> Earth around is sweeter green!
> Something lives in every hue
> Christless eyes have never seen:
> Birds with gladder songs o'erflow,
> Flow'rs with deeper beauties shine,
> Since I know, as now I know,
> I am His and He is mine."

Like children of the flesh, spiritual babies are a precious treasure to their Father. Few things delight our heavenly Father more than the simple trust of a newborn Christian. This is a time of rejoicing in heaven and of personal joy in the heart of the believer.

But this is also a time of great danger. The spiritual infant must not tarry too long in infancy, supinely savoring his happiness in Christ. He must proceed as quickly as possible to a program of spiritual growth. Otherwise he will be in great jeopardy from the hostile environment of the world.

Many childhood diseases can overtake the newborn babe in the family of God. One of the most dangerous is involvement with the cults.

In our time we have seen the happy results of evangelism in that millions have come to faith in Jesus Christ. The great and commendable efforts of the church and its gifted workers have produced many thousands of new converts to the Lord Jesus. The result is that there are great numbers of spiritual infants in the church at this time. Knowing this, the cults are thriving by pressing an ambitious program of infecting these blessed newborn souls with the deadly virus of false and destructive heresies.

It follows therefore that one of the great needs in the church today is for Christian growth. *Nothing* is more important than spiritual growth in the life of the newborn Christian. The spiritual babies mentioned in Scripture are called upon to "desire the sincere milk of the Word" that they may grow as a result.

The key to the development of Christian maturity is given us by the Apostle Paul in an admonition that should be heeded by us all. "All Scripture is given by inspiration of God, and is profitable for doctrine, for reproof, for correction, for instruction in righteousness; that the man of God may be perfect [mature], throughly furnished unto all good works" (2 Tim. 3:16-17).

The study of Holy Scripture and the consequent development toward Christian maturity is imperative for the new Christian. What is the key to spiritual growth? It is the study of the Word of God which produces the knowledge of sound doctrine.

3. Spiritual Subversion

Another reason sincere people are drawn off into the cults is that traveling religious carpetbaggers work industriously to subvert people from true faith in Jesus Christ into a religion that is contrary to the Word of God.

This was the case with a group of young Chris-

tians who had embraced the Gospel under the
ministry of the Apostle Paul in the province of
Galatia. Under his preaching, they responded to the
ministry of the grace of God with commendable
enthusiasm. Paul reminded them, "For I bear you
record, that, if it had been possible, ye would
have plucked out your own eyes, and have given
them to me" (Gal. 4:15). The ecstatic response of
the people in Galatia to his preaching must have
been a singular encouragement to the Apostle Paul.

We can therefore understand with what broken-
ness he must have written to the Galatians a short
time after this. He had heard of the spiritual subversion that was taking place in the lives of these
beloved Christians. He therefore exclaimed

> "I marvel that ye are so soon removed from Him
> that called you into the grace of Christ unto
> another gospel, which is not another, but there
> be some that trouble you, and would pervert the
> Gospel of Christ. But though we, or an angel
> from heaven, preach any other gospel unto you
> than that which we have preached unto you, let
> him be accursed. As we said before, so say I now
> again, 'If any man preach any other gospel unto
> you than that ye have received, let him be
> accursed'" (Gal. 1:6-9).

Certain representatives had come from Jerusalem and they were conducting a "follow-up"
ministry among the Galatians. They doubtless commended them for believing in the Gospel of the
grace of God but then proceeded to insist that they
must become obedient to the law of Moses in order
to be true Christians. Describing them Paul said,
"They zealously affect you, but not well" (Gal.
4:17). Quickly then Paul had to admonish the

Christians, "Stand fast therefore in the liberty wherewith Christ hath made us free, and be not entangled again with the yoke of bondage" (Gal. 5:1). Thus did Paul resist the **spiritual** subverters that were entering in like grievous wolves among the flock of the Galatians.

Spiritual subversion also took place among the Corinthians. The Corinthians were also infantile Christians (1 Cor. 3:1). As babes in Christ, they were vulnerable to those ubiquitous spirtual carpetbaggers that moved in to make merchandise of them. The subverters of the Corinthian Church were advocating the heresy of *phenomenalism*. That is, they were denying the Pauline thesis that the just shall live by faith and rather insisting that the just shall live by sight.

Concerning these enemies of the faith, Paul wrote to the Corinthians:

> "For such are false apostles, deceitful workers, transforming themselves into the apostles of Christ. And no marvel, for Satan himself is transformed into an angel of light. Therefore it is no great thing if his ministers also be transformed as the ministers of righteousness, whose end shall be according to their works" (2 Cor. 11:13-15).

Following this, Paul, with a sense of astonishment, says, "For ye suffer [allow it] if a man bring you into bondage, if a man devour you, if a man take of you, if a man exalt himself, if a man smite you on the face" (2 Cor. 11:20). Paul is speaking against the terrible spiritual vulnerability of these infantile Christians. Being weak and spineless, they allowed themselves to be knocked around and exploited by any new spiritual pretender who would move into their midst.

The church of the Colossians was also the object of the spiritual carpetbaggers who attempted to corrupt theologically this outpost of Christian liberty. The troublemakers came preaching the mysterious gnostic heresy. Therefore Paul said, "Beware lest any man spoil you through philosophy and vain deceit, after the tradition of men, after the rudiments of the world, and not after Christ" (Col. 2:8). He followed this by saying, "Let no man beguile you of your reward in a voluntary humility and worshiping of angels, intruding into those things which he hath not seen, vainly puffed up by his fleshly mind" (Col. 2:18).

During the apostolic era, it is probable that no church in the New Testament escaped the dreadful attention of the traveling servants of Satan who saw in these young congregations the opportunity to operate like a disguised wolf in a sheepfold. We may be sure that few churches of our present day will escape the like attention of similar spiritual opportunists.

4. Intellectual Pride

Another reason mentioned in the New Testament for defection from Christ and involvement in false religion is that pride of intellect to which all of us may be susceptible. This attitude among the Corinthians made it the more easy for the spiritual subverters to steal their affections from Christ. Paul wrote:

> "But I fear, lest by any means, as the serpent beguiled Eve through his subtilty, so your minds should be corrupted from the simplicity that is in Christ. For if he that cometh preacheth another Jesus, whom we have not preached, or if ye

receive another spirit, which ye have not received,
or another gospel, which ye have not accepted,
ye might well bear with him" (2 Cor. 11:3-4).

The Gospel is supposed to be believed with "simplicity and godly sincerity, not with fleshly wisdom,
but by the grace of God" (2 Cor. 1:12).

Intellectual pride has led many to feel that Christianity is "not sophisticated enough" or "too simple"
for their perceptive intellects. They are embarrassed at the invitation to come as a little child to
Christ and to continue to be a humble seeker after
truth. They are "vainly puffed up in their own
fleshly mind" as was the case with some of those in
the Colossian Church. Such people resent the Scripture which says:

"For it is written, 'I will destroy the wisdom of
the wise, and will bring to nothing the understanding of the prudent.' Where is the wise?
Where is the scribe? Where is the disputer of this
world? Hath not God made foolish the wisdom
of this world? For after that in the wisdom of
God the world by wisdom knew not God, it
pleased God by the foolishness of preaching to
save them that believe" (1 Cor. 1:19-21).

Each of us does well never to forget the advice
of Job, the wise patriarch of the Old Testament,
who said, "Behold, the fear of the Lord, that is
wisdom; and to depart from evil is understanding"
(Job 28:28). True wisdom consists in simple obedience to God and His Word.

Nevertheless the fact remains that for these and
many other reasons the cults continue to grow in
numbers and influence in Western Civilization. Volumes could be written to analyze the distinctive

delusions of the nearly endless list of individual cults in existence in our time. Surely the better course would be to consider the typical deficiencies of the cults. With these in mind, we may better recognize a cult, however new, as being a religious deviation condemned in Scripture.

There are not enough hours in a lifetime to read all the material that is being produced by those who believe something other than the Gospel of Jesus Christ. One does not need to do this but rather may be sure that if a religion under consideration is deficient in the following points, it is indeed a cult.

The first responsibility each Christian has is not to be an expert on the cults, but on the Word of God. Few pursuits are more exhausting than the attempt to get to the bottom of the endless labyrinth of cult pronouncements. One may avoid this pointless activity by remembering that if a religious view bears the following characteristics, it does not merit further study and can be dismissed as another gospel, not the faith of Christ.

A cultic religious point of view may be valuable in many ways and even true in part. This is what makes it attractive to its followers. What makes a religious practice a cult, however, is not only the falsities which it believes but also its fatal omissions of sound doctrine.

The following chapters present generally common characteristics, one or more of which is descriptive of the cults in existence today.

2 | Extra-Biblical Revelation

How has God revealed Himself?

The Christian answer to that question is that God has revealed Himself "on many occasions in diverse manners" in days gone by. In these last days, however, He has revealed Himself fully and finally to us in Jesus Christ as revealed in the Bible, the Word of God (see Heb. 1:1-2).

The Word of God is, therefore, God's final and complete revelation, and this revelation can be supplanted by no other. The cults have no such commitment, believing in the heretical doctrine of extra-biblical revelation. They claim that God has spoken and recorded words, through whatever medium, *since* He gave us the New Testament Scriptures. They assert that God speaks or has spoken outside or apart from the Bible.

The first and most typical characteristic of a cult

is that it claims for its authority some revelation apart from the clear statements of the Word of God. Most cults claim to respect the teachings of the Bible. Many even attribute divine inspiration to Holy Scripture. They then quickly announce their real confidence in some subsequent revelation that in effect cancels the teaching of the Bible in favor of a more authoritative new thing which they claim God has spoken subsequently. They are therefore claiming that the Bible is only a part of the verbal revelation of God and that He has spoken or does speak in a manner that is extra-biblical, apart from Scripture.

One Los Angeles based religious cult recently advertised:

> "The Bible has become to you the Book, but I would also have you know that God has inspired men and women with power to reveal, in our own time, even greater things, and ever fresh unfoldings from the heart of life.

> "Above all things, we want you to have the open vision today, for greater things are coming, and God is doing wonders among you. Rejoice in the new revelation, abounding in hope. The new will reveal the old to you afresh. Have no doubts. Launch out into the deeps of God, and fear not. Eternity is now."

Sometimes this extra-biblical revelation comes in the form of a "divinely inspired leader." Many religions have invested divine authority in the person of a visible individual who speaks infallibly, his words having the same or higher authority than Holy Scripture. Some of these religions have made their leaders equal with God.

From "Brother Julius" in Brooklyn to a spiritual

temple in Los Angeles, the cults continue to press for a better revelation than the Word of God. William Branham, in his *Word to the Bride*, said, "One night as I was seeking the Lord, the Holy Spirit told me to pick up my pen and write. As I grasped the pen to write, His Spirit gave me a message for the church. I want to bring it to you . . . . It has to do with the Word and the bride."

The God of the Bible, knowing that this would be the case in the future of the Church, very clearly declares His Word, the Scriptures, to be final and unsupersedable revelation. After giving us 66 books in the Old and New Testaments, the Holy Spirit directed the Apostle John to categorically close the verbal revelation of God at the conclusion of the Bible, saying, "For I testify unto every man that heareth the words of the prophecy of this book, if any man shall add unto these things, God shall add unto him the plagues that are written in this book; and if any man shall take away from the words of the book of this prophecy, God shall take away his part out of the book of life" (Rev. 22: 18-19).

Clearly then, we have in Scripture a dreadful curse placed upon anyone who presumes to present a new verbal revelation from God.

In a frantic attempt at rationalization, some cultists say, "Well, our revelation did not come from the word of man but from a higher source." The Mormons' claim to the coming of an angel is an illustration of this.

As if foreseeing this, the Apostle Paul wrote, "But though we, or an angel from heaven, preach any other gospel unto you than that which we have preached unto you, let him be accursed. As we said before, so say I now again, 'If any man preach any other gospel unto you than that ye have received, let him be accursed' " (Gal. 1:8-9).

It is true that in biblical times the Word was carried to man by angels (Heb. 2:2). We are told, however, that the revelation of Jesus Christ supersedes this. "God, who at sundry times and in divers manners spake in time past unto the fathers by the prophets, hath in these last days spoken unto us by His Son, whom He hath appointed heir of all things, by whom also He made the worlds" (Heb. 1:1-2).

Christ is better than the angels, and all of the angels of God are commanded to worship Him. The final words of Scripture, therefore, "the revelation of Jesus Christ," can never be superseded by the ministry of angels. This is why Jesus Christ advised His disciples and us to "continue in My word" (John 8:31). Our present age is also well advised to heed the words of the Father, "This is my beloved Son . . . hear ye Him" (Matt. 17:5).

It is a cardinal doctrine of Christianity that final truth, the ultimate word is resident in Jesus Christ. Indeed the Scripture is itself even stronger than that, saying, "In the beginning was the Word, and the Word was with God, and the Word *was* God" (John 1:1).

Final truth therefore *is* the Person, the Word, and the work of Jesus Christ. No subsequent revelation as to the nature of truth can supersede the revelation of Jesus Christ. It is simply impossible for there to be a greater revelation than that of Christ in this universe or any other under the God who made this and all possible universes.

One frequent device of a cult is to lend credence

to its own writings by placing them parallel to the Scriptures and then moving them up to a greater authority.

"The revealed scriptures predict the genuine incarnations of God well in advance of their earthly appearances. For instance, the Old Testament predicted the appearance of Lord Jesus Christ, and Srimad-Bhagavatam predicted the appearance of Lord Buddha, Lord Caitanya Mahaprabhu, and even Lord Kalki, who will not appear for another 400,000 years. Without reference to such bona fide scriptural predictions, no incarnation of the Lord can be bona fide. Indeed, the scriptures warn that in this age there will be many false incarnations. Lord Jesus Christ cautioned his followers that in the future many imposters would claim to be him. Similarly, Srimad-Bhagavatam also warns of false incarnations, describing them to be just like glowworms imitating the moon. Modern imposters often claim that their ideas represent the same teachings taught by Christ or Krsna, but anyone truly familiar with the teachings of Christ or Krsna can easily see that this is just nonsense" (*Back to Godhead,* No. 61, 1974, p. 24).

So it is that the Krishna cult, the modern followers of His Divine Grace A. C. Bhaktivedanta Swami Prabhupada, grasp for authority in the minds of the foolish. They place their arcane and mysterious writings on a par with the Word of God.

A word of admonition is therefore in order. The Christian believes the Bible to be the final and only verbal revelation of God. Believing this, he must give himself to the study of the Word of God with a higher degree of intensity than ever before.

The subtle assaults being leveled against the Scripture in these days need to be answered by articulate Christians in all walks of life. It is not enough for us to hold the Bible in tranquil veneration, looking at it with great admiration as the touchstone of our faith. The Bible is "the sword of the Spirit" and will become for us an effective instrument against satanic assaults when we build the teaching of Holy Scripture into the very fiber of our personal beings.

One is at least being inconsistent and perhaps hypocritical if he professes a high view of Scripture but neglects to dispel his ignorance of the truth of God through a serious program of Bible study. *The greatest single reason for the advance of the cults in our world today is ignorance of Holy Scripture on the part of Christians.* The second greatest is unwillingness on the part of the people of God to transmit divine truth by way of a testimony for Christ to others who need yet to receive salvation in Christnor.

It follows that the great need in the Christian community in our time is a return to a careful study of the Word of God. Faith that the Bible is ultimate truth will come from that very program of Bible study. A study of Scripture will produce in the life of the Christian the fulfillment of the promise, "Faith cometh by hearing, and hearing by the word of God" (Rom. 10:17).

It is a truism that truth bears its own credentials to the honest mind. No one will doubt the final authority of the Word of God who gives himself to the attentive study of Bible doctrine and memorization of Scripture. The fearful assault upon the Church by aroused and powerful cults will only be withstood when Christians are made strong in the Lord by a knowledge of His Word.

David hid the Word of God in his heart in order that he might resist the sinful alternatives of life (see Ps. 119:11). This means he memorized portions of the Bible, and so should we.

The life of a Christian will be firmly anchored against all opposition when it is grounded in a working knowledge of Holy Scripture.

3 | A False Basis of Salvation

What must I do to be saved? Deep within his heart, virtually every person on earth is asking this question first phrased by the Philippian jailor. Man is born with an unquenchable longing for eternal life and a home in heaven that will never pass away. Millions may never admit to this longing but, nevertheless, within each soul is the constantly pressing desire for a secure eternal reality, a hope that goes beyond the grave.

This longing for reality is the fuel that energizes the growth of most of the cults in existence today. Because they are involved in some form of exploitation, the cults without exception obscure the truth and offer salvation on some other basis than that of a free gift that comes to us by the grace of Jesus Christ.

What is the true basis of salvation?

The clear teaching of the New Testament Scriptures is that eternal salvation comes to a believer solely as a result of faith in Jesus Christ. The New Testament Scriptures declare again and again this sublime Christian truth.

"Therefore being justified by faith, we have peace with God through our Lord Jesus Christ" (Rom. 5:1).

"For all have sinned, and come short of the glory of God, being justified freely by His grace through the redemption that is in Christ Jesus, whom God hath set forth to be a propitiation through faith in His blood, to declare His righteousness for the remission of sins that are past, through the forbearance of God" (Rom. 3:23-25).

"Therefore we conclude that a man is justified by faith without the deeds of the law" (Rom. 3:28).

"Now to him that worketh is the reward not reckoned of grace, but of debt. But to him that worketh not, but believeth on Him that justifieth the ungodly, his faith is counted for righteousness" (Rom. 4:4-5).

"Knowing that a man is not justified by the works of the law, but by the faith of Jesus Christ, even we have believed in Jesus Christ, that we might be justified by the faith of Christ, and not by the works of the law; for by the works of the law shall no flesh be justified" (Gal. 2:16).

"For by grace are ye saved through faith, and that not of yourselves, it is the gift of God, not of works, lest any man should boast" (Eph. 2:8-9).

These and many other clear declarations of the New Testament positively establish the basis of salvation to be the finished work of Christ alone and our faith in that work.

By contrast, Scripture teaches that all other forms of supposed salvation, based on human efforts, are cursed by God. "For as many as are of the works of the law are under the curse; for it is written, 'Cursed is every one that continueth not in all things which are written in the book of the law to do them.' But that no man is justified by the law in the sight of God, it is evident; for, 'The just shall live by faith'" (Gal. 3:10-11).

How wonderful is the message of the Gospel of the grace of God that is presented to us in Holy Scripture! A person is able to come to Jesus Christ without money, without human works, without vast promises concerning the future and accept salvation which was entirely purchased for him on the cross. When he comes in humble faith, he receives the *gift* of God which is eternal life. And it is exactly this, a free gift. When he believes the Gospel, he receives eternal life and is justified in the sight of God.

To be justified, of course, means to be *declared* righteous. This is a legal change in the attitude of God toward the sinner and depends on the saving act of Jesus Christ which is entirely independent of the individual experience of the believer. The wonderful change which may result in a believer's life is not itself salvation but rather the human and variable *result* of that saving faith. Eternal salvation comes to the believer because of *imputed* righteousness. Imputed righteousness is righteousness that is placed to his account in heaven.

During the course of a Christian's life, he may develop a wonderful degree of personal righteousness. In this, he will have the powerful help of the indwelling Holy Spirit of God. The true believer will work toward perfect holiness in the fear of God under the leadership of the Holy Spirit.

Personal righteousness is not, however, the basis of his salvation. He is saved on the basis of *imputed* righteousness. This comes to him as a free gift, being purchased by the enormous cost of the finished work of Christ on Calvary's cross. The Christian is saved, not because of his own works but because of the saving work of Jesus Christ when Christ the Saviour died, the Just for the unjust, that He might bring us to God (1 Peter 3:18). The total benefits of Calvary come to the believer on the basis of grace. It is the grace of God that brings salvation.

No message is more viciously attacked by the cult promoters of our present world than the Gospel of the grace of God. Those who would promote slavish religious systems are infuriated at the gracious offer of Jesus Christ to bring His life into the sin-darkened soul and to do it without any form of payment. It is absolutely maddening to the professional religious promoters that God saves individuals freely, by grace alone.

No false religion in the world can possibly survive unless it is able to destroy the Gospel of the grace of God and introduce or encourage a system of human works as a basis of salvation. There is not room in the same world for the Pauline message of "justification by faith without the deeds of the law" and the cultic religionist with his perverted gospel. Every cult in the world preaches "another gospel" and is therefore cursed of God.

Nevertheless, the promoters of the cults continue to press their malignant doctrines of some other way of salvation besides faith in the finished work of Christ on the cross.

One of the most popular alternative doctrines of salvation is that of salvation by membership. Armstrong's Worldwide Church of God clearly announces that the only saved people are those who are members of this increasingly shaky religious establishment.

Pseudo Christianity in many forms has frequently announced that "there is no salvation outside of the church," meaning of course their religious syndicate. Failure to keep this membership intact incurs the damnation of the soul.

Others offer even stranger salvation promises such as salvation by sublime association. The new Krishna devotees are told:

> "Therefore one who is sufficiently intelligent will associate with saintly persons who are free from the entanglement of material nature and who can sever the knots which bind. There is no benefit in associating with those who are simply engaged in sense gratification. If we want liberation, if we really want to get out of this illusory existence, we must associate with *mahatmas*, great souls. All we have to do is simply hear, *sravanam*, and by simply hearing from great souls our knot of nescience will be cut. Just hearing Hare Krsna, Hare Krsna, Krsna Krsna, Hare Hare / Hare Rama, Hare Rama, Rama Rama, Hare Hare will save us" (*Back to Godhead*, No. 46, "We Belong to Krsna," p. 7).

Another alternative to the way of faith is the cult doctrine of salvation by works. In many of these religious programs, what a person *believes* is of little consequence; it is what he *does* that counts.

The versions of this works doctrine are many. Some emphasize years of service, weekly hours spent in work, the giving of money, the practice of strange incantations, the reciting of chants; the list is endless. There is an immense number of possible obligations to which the soul enslaves itself when it turns from the divine offer of salvation by faith alone.

The pathetic followers of the Jehovah's Witnesses are told that the basis of judgment at the end of the 1,000 years will be solely the works that they perform during the millennium.

The Christian Scientists are asked to believe that salvation consists of being saved from the illusions and delusions of mortal sense . . . the sense of becoming sick and dying.

In the early days of Mormonism, the Mormon women accepted the staggering involvement in polygamy because they became convinced that their salvation depended on it.

The Unitarians believe in salvation by character, holding that man will find the road that leads to peace and brotherhood through development of "moral values and spiritual insights."

The followers of Theosophy hold that man is saved by working out his own "karma" or law works. What he is now is the result of previous works and what he is to become is the result of his present works.

The list is seemingly endless of those who are pursuing inner light, perfect realization, transcendental thoughts, or other baseless notions as the hope of salvation. All of these human works must inevitably lead to despair.

By contrast to all of this we need to hear again

the finality of the words of Paul, "If righteousness come by the law, then Christ is dead in vain" (Gal. 2:21). Proud men who still retain confidence in their ability to do good things that will be pleasing to God and produce salvation need again to hear the words of Jesus Christ, "None of you keepeth the law" (John 7:19).

There is no question but that every false cult will lead finally to human despair, death, and hell. Millions could be saved from this spiritual tragedy if they would turn in simple confidence to the promise of Scripture, "Believe on the Lord Jesus Christ, and thou shalt be saved" (Acts 16:31). Few scenes are more tragic than that of a benighted soul pursuing a false hope of salvation when Jesus Christ offers all of this as a free gift.

4 | Uncertain Hope

The soul that is in distress is also in bondage!

If a person's distress can be perpetuated by a religious promoter, that promoter can be reasonably sure of keeping a distressed soul in continued and ever increasing bondage. The religious charlatan, therefore, must be very careful never to produce a final cure. Rather he must push certainty up into an unrealizable future in order to keep needy souls continually striving today.

We ought not to be surprised, therefore, that a nearly universal characteristic of the cults of our time is their insistence that one can never be sure of eternal life while in this world. The issue of salvation is never settled. The follower lives in constant fear that he has not done enough, given enough, prayed enough, worshiped enough to be sure of salvation.

One suspects because of all of this that the cults are really not talking about salvation at all, but rather are pushing religious philosophies tied to a set of unrealizable goals in the name of which they can extract every kind of sacrifice from their hapless followers.

The atheist Robert Ingersoll came close to describing leadership in programs like this when he said, "A preacher is one who is willing to take care of your affairs in the next world providing you will support him in this one." This is a cynical but apt description of the false religious leader who is not really interested in producing the assurance of salvation. He would be out of business very quickly if he set people free. His support would cease.

The cult promoters, being interested in only the fulfillment of their lust for power, money, or satisfaction, are very careful to extract from their followers a response today in return for a promise which can only be fulfilled tomorrow. Uncertainty is a favorite cult weapon. It would hardly be possible to promote a successful cult if one offered the assurance of salvation or any sure hope of eternal life based upon the finished work of another.

The wonderful promise of the New Testament is in contrast to all of this. The Bible promises to the believing Christian that he is the possessor of a certain salvation. "Blessed be the God and Father of our Lord Jesus Christ, which according to His abundant mercy hath begotten us again unto a lively hope by the resurrection of Jesus Christ from the dead, to an inheritance incorruptible, and undefiled, and that fadeth not away, reserved in heaven for you, who are kept by the power of God through faith unto salvation ready to be revealed in the last time. Wherein ye greatly rejoice" (1 Peter 1:3-6).

The Christian is "sealed with that Holy Spirit of promise" (Eph. 1:13). He is the possessor of hope, both sure and stedfast (Heb. 6:19).

The cultists make no such promise. Because they are interested in producing perpetual obligation as against spiritual freedom, they keep their followers in the hopeless bondage of a continually insecure relationship with God. For the member of the cult there is always more to do, more to pay, and his hope of blessing in eternal life is a will-o'-the-wisp that can never be certainly realized in this life. A hope so uncertain is hardly a hope at all.

The Jehovah's Witnesses promise the new birth to only their inner 144,000. No one knows quite who constitutes this inner group or what will be the destiny of those outside of it.

The followers of Theosophy are pursuing a set of philosophies so abstract that they produce no assurance at all.

Edgar Cayce promises assurance only in some future life, saying, "Since we all have sinned and come short of the glory of God, we would be doomed if we only had one *life* for making ourselves acceptable for the Father."

Pursuers of the inner peace movement risk despair on days in which their inner peace is less "real" to them than before.

The Krishna crowd pursues a relativistic emergence into divinity in which no one can be certain where he stands at a given moment. They promise that if you live a life of Krishna consciousness then, when you leave your body, if you think of him you will achieve bliss.

A thoughtful person who examines the preaching and writing of the cults carefully is almost certain to sense a frustrating indefiniteness. He is being strung along, beguiled up a primrose path to nowhere.

A common characteristic of the cults is that they are devoid of a theological structure that offers to anyone a sure salvation. It would be unthinkable for them to ever say in the words of Scripture, "For I am persuaded that neither death, nor life, nor angels, nor principalities, nor powers, nor things present, nor things to come, nor height, nor depth, nor any other creature shall be able to separate us from the love of God, which is in Christ Jesus our Lord" (Rom. 8:38-39).

What a blessed contrast we have to this trembling cultic fear in the words of this same Apostle Paul, "I know whom I have believed, and am persuaded that He is able to keep that which I have committed unto Him against that day" (2 Tim. 1:12).

Paul's absolute certainty of eternal life is revealed in the many statements of confidence that he expressed as to his sure hope of heaven.

"For we know that if our earthly house of this tabernacle were dissolved, we have a building of God, an house not made with hands, eternal in the heavens" (2 Cor. 5:1).

"For I am in a strait betwixt two, having a desire to depart, and to be with Christ, which is far better" (Phil. 1:23).

"For our conversation is in heaven; from whence also we look for the Saviour, the Lord Jesus Christ, who shall change our vile body, that it may be fashioned like unto His glorious body, according to the working whereby He is able even to subdue all things unto Himself" (Phil. 3:20-21).

"Who hath delivered us from the power of darkness, and hath translated us into the kingdom of His dear Son" (Col. 1:13).

"When Christ, who is our life, shall appear, then shall ye also appear with Him in glory" (Col. 3:4).

"Then we which are alive and remain shall be caught up together with them in the clouds, to meet the Lord in the air; and so shall we ever be with the Lord" (1 Thes. 4:17).

By contrast to the obscure future that is the best the cult can offer, Paul brightly tells us that Christ "hath abolished death, and hath brought life and immortality to light through the Gospel" (2 Tim. 1:10).

We may be very sure that the promoter of a false religion who is interested in producing dependence upon himself as against freedom that comes through faith in Christ would never pass on to his followers the words of Christ, "My sheep hear My voice, and I know them, and they follow Me; And I give unto them eternal life; *and they shall never perish*, neither shall any man pluck them out of My hand. My Father, which gave them Me, is greater than all; and no man is able to pluck them out of My Father's hand" (John 10:27-29).

It is interesting to note that the verse immediately following this promise says, "Then the Jews took up stones again to stone Him." Natural men, even in the realm of religious leadership, will do anything to destroy the perfect confidence that a relationship with Jesus Christ brings to a life. The reason is very clear, *they traffic in anxiety*.

The person who is anxious is also exploitable. To make him fearful is the design of these religious leaders so that they may use fear to create dependence upon the religious view that they are promoting. Cult gathering places are populated by frightened people who live in terror of falling into the disfavor of their religious establishment. Our modern society is not without many tragic wrecks of humanity whose psychic nature has been shattered, their confidence destroyed as a result of a previous total involvement in a false religion.

To any such, we happily repeat the wonderful promise, "If the Son therefore shall make you free, ye shall be free indeed" (John 8:36).

5 | Presumptuous Messianic Leadership

Only Jesus Christ deserves disciples!

This towering fact is ignored by most of the religions in the world today.

The Christian message is that Jesus Christ is the Author and Finisher of our faith (Heb. 12:2). He alone is our High Priest (Heb. 4:14). He alone is our Mediator (1 Tim. 2:5). The Church is the body of Christ, of which He is the head (Eph. 1:22-23).

To the Christian, Jesus Christ is all in all (Col. 3:11). We have a telling example of this in that gracious individual whom God called to be a forerunner of Jesus Christ, John the Baptist. Because of his remarkable ministry, John became the object of great spiritual interest. This spiritual interest produced a following. Many potential followers of John asked questions which implied that they would want to attribute to him some divine qualities, making him their leader. What was the Baptist's answer? The Apostle John gives us the most fascinating account:

> "And this is the record of John, when the Jews sent priests and Levites from Jerusalem to ask him, 'Who art thou?' And he confessed, and denied not; but confessed, 'I am not the Christ.' And they asked him, 'What then? Art thou Elias?' And he saith, 'I am not.' 'Art thou that prophet?' And he answered, 'No.' Then said they unto him, 'Who art thou? that we may give an answer to them that sent us. What sayest thou of thyself?' He said, 'I am the voice of one crying in the wilderness, "Make straight the way of the Lord," as said the prophet Esaias'" (John 1:19-23).

When asked these questions, John the Baptist may well have been tempted to at least be a bit mysterious about his true nature. How delightful is his instant, honest response, "I am not the Christ." "No, no, no" was the form of his emphatic denial of any messianic quality. He insisted on exalting Jesus Christ, saying, "This was He of whom I spake, 'He that cometh after me is preferred before me; for He was before me'" (John 1:15).

John the Baptist left us a most commendable example by constantly deferring from the praise and applause of the fawning humanity that gathered about him. Later, there were those who came to inform John that "all men" were coming and following Jesus Christ. John's answer is the essence of humility:

> "A man can receive nothing, except it be given him from heaven. Ye yourselves bear me witness,

that I said, 'I am not the Christ, but that I am sent before Him.' He that hath the bride is the bridegroom, but the friend of the bridegroom, which standeth and heareth him, rejoiceth greatly because of the bridegroom's voice; this my joy therefore is fulfilled. He must increase, but I must decrease" (John 3:27-30).

"He must increase—I must decrease."

How fearful is the contrast of the life and ministry of many religious leaders in our time. The cults are replete with the stated or implied suggestion on the part of leaders as to some unusual divine capability that might well inspire worship on the part of their followers.

In 1954, Sun Myung Moon founded the "Holy Spirit Association for the Unification of World Christianity." This Korean millionaire religious promoter claims 600,000 followers worldwide and fosters in them the belief that he is the "Lord of the Second Advent," the personalized second coming of Jesus Christ. Moon rose out of his Presbyterian and Pentecostal background to organize a cult around a new theology that presents him as the great hope for mankind. He and his second wife are put forth as the new Adam and Eve, and their followers are the first children of a new and perfect world.

Judge Rutherford of the Jehovah's Witnesses presented himself as "God's chosen vessel" and the Watchtower organization as the final dispenser of truth.

Joseph Smith of the Mormons claimed that John the Baptist had given to him the priesthood of Aaron. As if this were not enough, he later claimed that he had received a higher priesthood, that of Melchizedek, from Peter, James, and John. His followers repeatedly claim that he has done more for the salvation of this world than any other man who has ever lived, except Jesus.

L. Ron Hubbard of the Scientology cult has offered himself as a higher authority than Jesus Christ or the Christian Bible. This science fiction writer has produced a devoted set of followers who press millions of dollars into his hands.

Guru Maharaj Ji has presented himself as the "perfect master" and the "lord of the universe" and is esteemed as such by his thousands of followers across America and the world. It is ironic that this exalted personality, being a juvenile, had to get permission from a local judge to marry his 24-year-old secretary.

Meher Baba of the Bahai cult has said, "There is no doubt of my being God personified .... I am the Christ .... I assert unequivocally that I AM infinite consciousness; I make this assertion because I AM infinite consciousness. I am everything and I am beyond everything. . . . Before me was Zoroaster, Krishna, Rama, Buddha, Jesus, and Mohammad .... My present avataric form is the last incarnation of the cycle of time, hence my manifestation will be the greatest."

One of the marks of a cult is that it elevates the person and the words of a human leader to a messianic level. The predictable characteristic of a member of a cult is that he will soon be quoting his leader, whether Father Divine, Prophet Jones, Mary Baker Eddy, Judge Rutherford, Herbert Armstrong, or Buddha as a final authority. A messianic human leader has used the powers of his intelligence or personality and with them imposed his ideas and directives on the ignorant.

The success of this approach is usually predictable, for too many religiously disposed people are not intellectually responsible enough to think for themselves. Their easy mental acquiescence has led them to seek a leader who can give them all of the answers and personalize or objectify their religious need. They want someone to speak to them with authority, even finality.

All too often converts to a religion stand in inordinate awe of the person who brought them into that faith. Many religious persuaders have been unable to withstand the temptation to personally promote themselves so as to retain their exalted image in the minds of their devoted followers. The temptation to change from a simple servant to an exalted messiah can be very strong in the life of a charismatic leader.

It is possible that many cult organizers began as humble people who came to believe their own promotion. They soon stamped their names on everything and pushed themselves as being utterly indispensable to the faith of their followers. They then often cleverly continue to promote the image of external humility while in fact spending millions to keep their names in lights before their starry-eyed followers. "My people need me," is their assumption, "and, bless them, they can have me— for a price."

No Christian should make such a mistake. He is aware that all have sinned and come short of the glory of God. He knows that from the least to the greatest, each Christian, but for the grace, the *unmerited* favor of Jesus Christ, would be corrupt and lost. He remembers the apostle who said, "By the grace of God I am what I am" (1 Cor. 15:10).

The Christian has no final human leader except Jesus Christ. He is warned about this by Christ Himself who said, "But be not ye called Rabbi, for One is your Master, even Christ, and all ye are brethren. And call no man your father upon the earth, for One is your Father, which is in heaven. Neither be ye called masters, for One is your Master, even Christ. But he that is greatest among you shall be your servant" (Matt 23:8-11).

The followers of Christ are not masters of one another, but they relate to one another as members of a body. They are to serve one another (Gal. 5:13). They are to submit themselves to one another (1 Cor. 16:16). The Scriptures clearly declare that when they announce themselves as devoted followers of a human leader, they have sunk into carnality. "For ye are yet carnal; for whereas there is among you envying, and strife, and divisions, are ye not carnal, and walk as men? For while one saith, 'I am of Paul'; and another, 'I am of Apollos' [the list has expanded through the centuries]; are ye not carnal?" (1 Cor. 3:3-4) Even Paul, when writing to Timothy, humbly said, "Consider what I say; and the Lord give thee understanding in all things" (2 Tim. 2:7).

Any person therefore who professes to be a true Christian makes a mistake when he calls himself by the name of any human leader. Scripture says, "Ye are bought with a price; be not ye the servants of men" (1 Cor. 7:23). It is the duty of a Christian to glorify God (1 Cor. 6:20) and to exercise great discretion in giving honor to men.

Few of us will meet more than two or three truly great men in the whole of our lifetimes, and probably none under the age of 70. Notice, in this regard, how many "great" men of the Old Testament really had but a brief era of greatness and then died fools. The stories of Samson, David, Solomon, and many other great men of biblical and religious history are simply the stories of *humanity* in its truest form. That which is born of the flesh is flesh, and no mysterious self-deification will ever make it different.

The religious leader in our time must take great care in this regard. He must sternly prevent admirers from becoming enamored of his leadership rather than the leadership of Jesus Christ.

In this he is doing no more than following the example of our Lord, who "made Himself of no reputation, and took upon Him the form of a servant, and was made in the likeness of men; and being found in fashion as a man, He humbled Himself, and became obedient unto death, even the death of the cross" (Phil. 2:7-8). This same Lord Jesus said, "He that speaketh of himself seeketh his own glory" (John 7:18). Christ spoke of the chief religious leaders of His day most critically when He said, "For they loved the praise of men more than the praise of God" (John 12:43).

One who would aspire to be an effective servant of Jesus Christ must never forget the earnest words of his Lord, "Verily, verily, I say unto you, the servant is not greater than his lord; neither he that is sent greater than he that sent him. If ye know these things, happy are ye if ye do them" (John 13:16-17).

The person who seeks glory from a human following does well to remember the fickleness of the crowd. Paul had to write finally to his constituents at Galatia and say, "Am I therefore become your enemy because I tell you the truth?" (Gal. 4:16)

Jesus Christ warned us along those same lines, saying, "Woe unto you, when all men shall speak well of you! for so did their fathers to the false prophets" (Luke 6:26). He expanded on this theme, saying, "Blessed are ye, when men shall revile you, and persecute you, and shall say all manner of evil against you falsely, for My sake" (Matt. 5:11). It is clear, then, that the credential of a true servant of Jesus Christ is not the applause of the multitudes. Indeed, he must rather be willing to go outside the camp if necessary, bearing Christ's reproach.

Another form of presumptuous messianic leadership in the religious scene of our time is the claim of some leaders to their own ability as special intercessors with God. Their followers are asked by them to "believe in my prayers" and to "give me the opportunity to pray for you." There is a general build-up of presumption that the leader, because of his special gifts or deep spirituality, has some unusual powers with which to gain leverage before the throne of God. The claim to special prayer ability by the spiritual leader is a cruel device by which millions of sheeplike followers have been beguiled into servitude. Following this, they have been exploited to a frightening degree. This shameful doctrine is false and foreign to the teaching of the New Testament.

By contrast to the heretical view of "special prayer ability," Jesus spoke to *every* believer, saying, "Whatsoever you will ask in My name, that will I do" (John 14:13). Protestant Christianity was built on the sound biblical doctrine of the priesthood of every believer. The clear teaching of the New Testament is that each person who has been justified by faith in Jesus Christ has access to the Father in prayer and needs no human mediator.

The doctrine of the priesthood of every believer needs to be rediscovered and reemphasized in the Christian scene today. Without this emphasis on sound doctrine, the messianic tendency on the part of leaders to claim special favor with God will produce a new religious hierarchy more deadly than the one from which we have been delivered.

No one has an inside track with God except Jesus Christ! *No one* has any access at all to the Father without Jesus Christ and *in Him* we all are freely welcomed to the throne of grace. One of the great promises of the Bible to every believer is found in Paul's words to Timothy, "For there is one God, and one mediator between God and men, the man Christ Jesus" (1 Tim. 2:5).

The promise of the writer of the Book of Hebrews is a blessed source of confidence to every child of God. "Seeing then that we have a great High Priest, that is passed into the heavens, Jesus the Son of God, let us hold fast our profession. For we have not an high priest which cannot be touched with the feeling of our infirmities, but was in all points tempted like as we are, yet without sin. Let us therefore come boldly unto the throne of grace, that we may obtain mercy, and find grace to help in time of need" (Heb. 4:14-16).

Every believer in Jesus Christ is himself a priest and has access to the Father because of the work of our great High Priest, Jesus Christ. "Having therefore, brethen, boldness to enter into the holiest by the blood of Jesus, by a new and living way, which He hath consecrated for us, through the veil, that is to say, His flesh; and having an High Priest over the house of God, let us draw near with a true heart in full assurance of faith, having our hearts sprinkled from an evil conscience" (Heb. 10:19-22).

The believer who responds to this blessed invitation of Scripture will never again be subject to the presumptuous messianic leadership of someone who arrogantly claims a special prayer relationship with God. In time of trouble, he will no longer call some "prayer team" in a distant city but will move by a new and living way into the holy place with the Lord himself. Should he desire also the prayers of others, he can meet before the throne of grace with his humble Christian friends. Distant hands laid on stacks of letters are as nothing compared to present believers meeting in prayer with Jesus Christ before the throne of God.

When Paul prayed for believers, he prayed that they themselves would know the personal access that they had to God and the wonderful powers that were available to them by virtue of their personal relationship to the Lord. "Wherefore I also, after I heard of your faith in the Lord Jesus, and love unto all the saints, cease not to give thanks for you, making mention of you in my prayers, that the God of our Lord Jesus Christ, the Father of glory, may give unto you the spirit of wisdom and revelation in the knowledge of Him, the eyes of your understanding being enlightened, that ye may know what is the hope of His calling, and what the riches of the glory of His inheritance in the saints, and what is the exceeding greatness of His power to usward who believe, according to the working of His mighty power" (Eph. 1:15-19).

Further in the same epistle, Paul continues to pray that each of us "may be able to comprehend *with all saints* what is the breadth, and length, and depth, and height; and to know the love of Christ, which passeth knowledge" (Eph. 3:18-19). Who can escape noticing the humility and tender spiritual concern in the Apostle Paul as he labored to bring each individual believer to Christian maturity, into the full realization of the privileges that were his from the Lord.

Surely one of the great needs in the Church is a restatement and understanding of the individual destiny of the believer. The great relationship for the Christian is that personal one which he has between himself and his Lord. This relationship continues, made viable by the Holy Spirit who lives within the heart of every believer independent of any human mediator.

In true Christianity no priest, no witchdoctor, no counselor, no human intercessor is necessary between the heart of the believer and the heart of God. The Scripture promises to every believer, "Be careful for nothing; but in everything by prayer and supplication with thanksgiving *let your requests be made known unto God*" (Phil. 4:6).

So each believer is invited to develop a growing *personal* relationship with his Lord. The message of the New Testament is very clear. The course in the life of the believer must move from dependence on the leadership of humans to independence of that leadership in the direction of a growing personal relationship to the Lord Himself.

The fearful contrast is apparent in the cult scene

today as cult leaders labor to produce idolatrous dependence upon themselves. The mark of the cult leader is that he makes himself imperative in the lives of those who have become ensnared in his web. This tragic development is only made possible because of the ignorance on the part of many people as to the teaching of the Word of God. The message of Scripture is that the individual must not commit himself to "infallible" human leaders. Rather he must become a follower of Jesus Christ, who alone is the head of the Church.

When a human being, made in the image of God, becomes an other-oriented automaton in his religious life, he negates the purpose for which he was created. Divine cosmology is destroyed by religious concepts that produce servants of a human master as against true followers of Jesus Christ. This satanic tendency was forever refuted by Jesus Christ when He said, "It is written, 'Thou shalt worship the Lord thy God, and Him only shalt thou serve'" (Luke 4:8).

The cult leader also strengthens his presumptuous leadership by arrogating to himself the position of being the only repository of divine truth. He frequently talks about "my message, my revelation, my leadership, my people." In doing this, he is pushing the heretical proposition that he has been made the true custodian of some private revelation from God. Concerning this we have the clear word of Scripture that no Scripture is of any private interpretation (2 Peter 1:20).

True religious leaders should emulate the Apostle Paul, who was careful never to press his leadership to the place where he would control the lives of others. There are all too few leaders in the world of religion today who could say with him, "Not for that we have dominion over your faith, but are helpers of your joy; for by faith ye stand" (2 Cor. 1:24).

Paul was careful to remind each Christian that he himself possesses "wisdom, righteousness, sanctification, and redemption" in Jesus Christ. Beyond this, the believer, without the help of any guru, possesses everything else he needs. "And again, 'The Lord knoweth the thoughts of the wise, that they are vain.' Therefore let no man glory in men. For all things are yours, whether Paul, or Apollos, or Cephas, or the world, or life, or death, or things present, or things to come; all are yours; and ye are Christ's; and Christ is God's" (1 Cor. 3:20-23).

Every individual believer possesses divine truth for himself when he holds the Word of God in his hand. The function of true Christian leadership is to bring each child of God to the point of maturity where he can study the Bible for himself and be delivered of his need of perpetual dependence on a human teacher.

Only Jesus Christ deserves disciples.

6 | Doctrinal Ambiguity

If the trumpet give an uncertain sound, who shall prepare himself for the battle?

The answer to this biblical question is that many strange people will. Response may well come from multitudes of individuals as they move out from the dark haunts of personal failure and confusion. There are increasing multitudes of people living in our generation to whom uncertain sounds seem to be beautiful music. To them uncertainty is a form of certainty and ambiguity satisfies the mind more than anything specific.

It is no wonder then that these types are attracted to the ambiguous doctrines of cult religions. Doctrinal ambiguity is a mark of a cult. One of the very fascinating characteristics of the cults is the interesting and sometimes hilarious changes of doctrine through which they pass. Their doctrines are being continually altered in order to adapt themselves to new situations, arguments, or the whims of their leaders. They know nothing of the command of Scripture, "That we henceforth be no more children, tossed to and fro, and carried about with every wind of doctrine, by the sleight of men, and cunning craftiness, whereby they lie in wait to deceive" (Eph. 4:14). Scripture is clear that craftily changing doctrine is a cunning device used by those who prey upon the unwary.

The illustrations are many. During and after the days of Mary Baker Eddy, the Christian Science cult republished her book *Science and Health With Key to the Scriptures* nearly every year. The annual update made it possible for the glaring contradictions and preposterous doctrines of the past to be adapted to the new demands of the present.

Guru Maharaj Ji says, "Are you feeling thirsty? Can you see that photo of Lord Shiva? You see the water coming out from the top of his head? Drink that water. Drink, drink! Can you? You can't drink that water. It is a picture. You need everything living. If you have doubts, you cannot ask Lord Krishna questions. That's why you need a living Master, for the circumstances of the world today. When Jesus was here there were no nuclear bombs. But now there are nuclear bombs, and the Perfect Master, the Perfect Saviour, has come to save you from nuclear bombs."

This same 16-year-old religious leader was asked the question, "What part does mantra play in meditation?"

His clear precise answer was, "Nothing, nothing. It just makes your tongue in gears, that's all.

Makes your mind flicker into some other way, that's all. But mind is still flickering. When I say 'Ram, Rrrr-Aaaa-Ma,' three times my mind flickers in one word: 'Ram.' More flickering of your mind—no good, no help. That is the question I place before people: 'You say Ram today, but what were the people saying before Ram was born?' Chanting is an external thing. See?"

There is simply no way that the rational mind can make sense out of these expressions or this activity. The word "doctrine" has no meaning in the fever swamps of the mind which are inhabited by the cults, for doctrine means a systematic presentation and understanding of truth. The idea of doctrine is therefore virtually unique to organized Christianity.

By contrast what passes for doctrine in the cult is really a sub-rational set of disconnected thoughts and practices that only serve to confuse the mind and the emotions as well. God gave us emotions so that they might be the source of flavor, happiness, joy at the understanding of truth and the fulfillment of duty. Emotions were never intended to be an end in themselves and are totally untrustworthy as the custodians of truth. Any religion, therefore, that deliberately bypasses rational doctrinal understanding and seeks to build upon the emotions will inevitably deceive rather then enlighten.

The use of chants, the raising of hands along with the clanging of cymbals, the sing-song repetition of simple musical structures, the repeated, staccato articulation of any word that is supposed to represent God, joy, or peace—all of these practices are sub-rational. They are simply calculated to play on the limited strings of the emotional structure, creating what passes as a religious experience but is nothing more than a mindless emotional trauma. Christ declared that we are not heard because of our "much speaking." This is a suggestion that is regularly ignored by the cults, whose adherents are not really speaking to God anyhow.

The Krishna addicts are also big on chanting, holding that their tuneless incantations are the way to all knowledge and the key to salvation.

> "The chanting of the *maha-mantra*—Hare Krsna, Hare Krsna, Krsna Krsna, Hare Hare/ Hare Rama, Hare Rama, Rama Rama, Hare Hare—is the recommended process of self-realization in this age. *Man* means mind, and *tra* means deliverance. Therefore, a *mantra* is a chant meant to deliver the mind from all unwanted thoughts. *Maha* means great. The Hare Krsna *maha-mantra* is the great chanting to deliver the mind from all unwanted thoughts which keep us from realizing our true selves. Our consciousness is originally pure or Krsna consciousness, but now, due to association with material nature, our minds are filled with impure thoughts" (*Back to Godhead*; No. 46, p. 1).

This set of spiritual abstractions, resembling the Hinduism that has already brought poverty and despair to millions in India, is now being preached in the United States. The chief purveyor is "His Divine Grace A. C. Bhaktivedanta Swami Prabhupada," who is the spiritual master of the International Society for Krishna Consciousness.

His magazine "Back to Godhead" explains about Prabhupada, saying, "He has mercifully given the chanting of Hare Krsna to the world so that everyone may regain his original joyful consciousness and live in peace and happiness. By chanting these holy names, we reestablish our lost link with the Supreme and enjoy our real life, which is full of eternity, knowledge, and bliss. Srila Prabhupada has asked, 'Please chant these holy names of the Lord. Your life will become sublime.' "

The illustrations of doctrinal ambiguity from the old and the new cults are endless. Never in the history of the world have there been so many confused and contradictory religious propositions pressed upon people in the guise of truth. The mind reels in confusion at any attempt to understand with any logical comprehension the preaching and doctrinal system of modern-day cults.

This "mindlessness" of the cults is a most useful device. The cult promoters are not truly appealing to the mind but rather are attempting to set the mind aside and to appeal to a set of religious emotions. Devotees say to one another in effect, "Forget what he is saying, can't you *feel* the vibrations? Surely we are in divine presence as the guru is speaking to us."

This "divine presence" is always justified by calling it *higher* knowledge, *deeper* truth, or the use of some other adjective that excuses it from being the real thing. Converts are not urged to understand; rather it is recommended that they feel. Terms like "self-realization," along with concepts like love, peace, and joy are the expressions in which they traffic. The words of the cults are the products of a corrupted language. The words themselves have no real meaning. They have become emotional triggers connoting to you whatever you want them to mean. The cult promoters have denied the doctrine of objective value as relates to the words they use.

By contrast, our Lord Jesus Christ was very careful about the use of His words. The result is that those who heard went away saying that they had never heard anyone who spoke like this man spoke. Christ clearly warned us as to the utter importance of the proper use of words with real meaning, saying, "By thy words thou shalt be justified, and by thy words thou shalt be condemned" (Matt. 12:37).

The Word of God is therefore very careful to avoid ambiguity. The contrast between bewildering, ambiguous cult doctrines and true Christianity is a very marked one. Nothing is clearer than the call in Scripture to sound doctrine. In a thousand ways, the Scriptures of the New Testament commit themselves to a careful exposition of the truth of God.

Indeed, unlike the religions of the world, Christianity commits itself to careful details of all kinds. The Bible is filled with notations of cities, villages, rivers, dates, times, kings, and exact quotes of what many individuals have said. Like no book in all of the world, the Bible is a book of careful historic detail.

In addition to this, important theological propositions in the Bible are stated in many ways so that there can be simply no question about the meaning. So clear and broad is the presentation of the facts of the Gospel that Paul was able to say to Timothy, "But thou hast *fully known* my doctrine, manner of life, purpose, faith, longsuffering, charity, patience" (2 Tim. 3:10).

We see then that clarity of belief is one of the characteristics of true Christianity. Jesus said, "I am the light of the world; he that followeth Me shall not walk in darkness, but shall have the light of life" (John 8:12).

The Christian who studies the Word of God becomes spiritually mature, a defender of the faith, and able even to teach others. The clear doctrines of Holy Scripture can be understood to the point of certainty by faithful people as they are transmitted from person to person, place to place, and age to age. Paul wrote, "The things that thou hast heard of me among many witnesses, the same commit thou to faithful men, who shall be able to teach others also" (2 Tim. 2:2).

The Word of God clearly warns that "the time will come when they will not endure sound doctrine; but after their own lusts shall they heap to themselves teachers, having itching ears; and they shall turn away their ears from the truth, and shall be turned into fables" (2 Tim. 4:3-4).

Fables, predicted in Scripture, are one of the marks of a cult. One can listen endlessly to cultic representatives on radio and television and never be sure what they are talking about. They pose questions which they do not answer. One of the most mentally frustrating experiences in life is to attempt to decide exactly what a religious promoter meant by what he said. The answer cannot be found even by reading hundreds of pages of his literature. Rather, the reader is led into an ever deeper labyrinth of confusion.

This is the way they plan it; they intend to confuse, not to clarify. Being confused themselves, they only are able to throw dust in the air so that it gets in the eyes of others. It is almost impossible to understand what a Jehovah's Witness believes about God, biblical inspiration, eternity, and many other subjects.

Armstrong's attempt to define the nature of the Godhead is a study in obfuscation. One finally concludes that we are even to become a part of God, a frightening heresy indeed.

Who can comprehend what the Inner Peace Movement is really talking about?

The Processians have given us a mass of impenetrable confusions in their new definitions of God, the devil, Christ, and the Holy Spirit. One almost suspects they put them all on the same level.

The Unity people suggest that since God sees and understands perfectly, and sees no evil because there is no evil, we shall see clearly the unreality and futility of appearances of evil, to which, through a misunderstanding, men now attribute substance and reality. Soon they will deny the true humanity of humanity!

The tendency of the cults is to move away from the objective, categoric truth as taught in Scripture. They hide behind the trees in the endless forest of philosophic discussion. To them the process of discussion is itself the truth. Nothing can be resolved because all things are continually and everlastingly relative. These indeed are people who are "ever learning and never able to come to the knowledge of truth" (see 2 Tim. 3:7).

We have an illustration from the life of Christ concerning the difference between philosophic discussion and real truth. Christ was witnessing to the woman at the well. The real truth about herself was the last thing in the world which this woman wanted to face. As a result, she attempted to push the discussion up into the realm of the philosophical, lest Christ get down to the case of her five husbands and her present adulterous life.

One can almost hear her voice, dripping with pseudo-sophistication, as she says, "Sir, I perceive that Thou art a prophet. Our fathers worshiped in this mountain; and ye say, that in Jerusalem is the place where men ought to worship.

"Jesus saith unto her, 'Woman, believe Me, the hour cometh, when ye shall neither in this mountain, nor yet at Jerusalem, worship the Father. Ye worship ye know not what; we know what we worship; for salvation is of the Jews. But the hour cometh, and now is, when the true worshipers shall worship the Father in spirit and in truth; for the Father seeketh such to worship Him'" (John 4:19-23).

In most pointed fashion, Christ cut through the fog of meaningless verbiage and brought this woman face to face with reality. As with Nicodemus and many others, Christ would not allow this woman to get away from the burning issue of her personal need, which was a matter of life and death. She was soon rejoicing in the result because she believed in Christ and then became an earnest witness to the reality of His salvation.

So it is that the message of the Gospel of Christ is continually presented in the Word of God as the profoundly beautiful and simple story of the Christ who died and rose again in order that we by faith in Him might have everlasting life.

By contrast, the dark night of doctrinal obscurity has settled on many segments of the current religious establishment because of the obfuscations and contradictions of the confused representatives of religion. The individual who seeks after truth in our times does well to heed the words of Christ, "If any man walk in the day, he stumbleth not, because he seeth the light of this world. But if a man walk in the night, he stumbleth, because there is no light in him" (John 11:9-10).

The great need in the religious establishment of our time is for the candid preaching of sound doctrine as against the tantalizing sentences of those who never do quite get to the point. Thank God for the faithful Christian expositors of the Scriptures in our time (may their tribe increase!) who can truthfully say, "I kept back nothing that was profitable unto you, but have shown you, and have taught you publicly, and from house to house, testifying both to the Jews, and also to the Greeks, repentance toward God, and faith toward our Lord Jesus Christ" (Acts 20:20-21).

Ambiguity is the devil's gospel, whereas clarity is divine.

7 | The Claim of "Special Discoveries"

"I have found the secret!"

Few people are more fascinating than those who claim to have inside information on a given subject. Who of us as a child has not listened with breathless anticipation to stories told by older people of their experiences? The sea, mountain caves, or the Khyber Pass lived for us in the tales that were passed on to us by those raconteurs. Stories of talking animals or mysterious haunted houses were a part of our youthful pursuits of fantasy.

Children's stories which are known to be fantasy are one thing; fantasies purveyed as religious truth are quite another. There is nothing wrong with listening to a storyteller and, after a smile or a tear, going on to do something else. The wrong, indeed the insane course, is to fall down at his feet and worship him.

Fables that are known to be such are enjoyable little diversions in life. Religious fantasies that are presented as special spiritual discoveries are dangerous.

In every walk of life, from the world of investment to the world of religion, many have been conned out of their money, their eternal souls, or both by those who claim special knowledge from sources of information not commonly available. In this regard, the world of business is in many ways wiser than the world of religion. It is illegal for any person to purchase securities on the basis of "inside information" not generally available to the average investor on the street. We could wish that in the world of religion there were such a law.

Unfortunately, such a law would be impossible to pass. Even if it were enacted, it would be ignored by millions of people in pursuit of religious fascinations rather than common truth.

The careful teacher of sound doctrine is rarely as electrifying as the mysterious religious promoter who, usually for a price, will let us in on his "secret." Under the spells he casts, we are often tempted to forget that the best things in life are not only free, but they are usually obvious.

The beauty of nature and the wonderful works of God are apparent to us on every hand. From an examination of these, we can discover our Lord's eternal power and Godhead (Rom. 1:20). From a serious study of His Word, the Holy Bible, we have available to us everything in life, without exception.

How wonderful is the promise of the Word of God! "According as His divine power hath given unto us all things that pertain unto life and godliness, through the knowledge of Him that hath called us to glory and virtue; whereby are given unto us exceeding great and precious promises, that by these ye might be partakers of the divine nature, having escaped the corruption that is in the world through lust" (2 Peter 1:3-4).

It is very clear that the humble Christian who will pursue the teaching of the Bible with simplicity and godly sincerity becomes the glad recipient of the abundant provision of God for every need for time and eternity. There can be no greater promise than that we are blessed "with all spiritual blessings in heavenly places in Christ" (Eph. 1:3).

In the face of this open provision of all things freely given from God, one is amazed to see the large and loyal following that comes to people who report some vision, presence, revelation, or special discovery which has come to them and which they claim to be divine. It would be impossible to have a cult without mysterious, otherwise unavailable inside information. In one way or another, each of these dreadful religions traffics in such hallucinations.

The Christian must remember that there is no discovery in the entire universe that anyone could possibly have that is superior to his discovery of salvation in Jesus Christ. There is no higher information, no better revelation, no deeper truth—nothing is greater than the knowledge of Christ. The person who turns from this greatest discovery, this ultimate revelation, to pursue the delusions of a cult leader is a fool. Despite this obvious truth, the cults continue to beguile unstable souls with their false claims to special discoveries. No discovery is more special than Jesus Christ.

The British Israelists claim to have discovered the marvelous truth that the Anglo-Saxon Celtic people are the 10 lost tribes of Israel. They claim that Elizabeth II actually sits on the throne of King David of Israel. She is his direct descendant and continues his dynasty, sitting also on the very throne on which Christ shall sit after His return to earth.

Foolish Americans and Englishmen, some of them famous as well as foolish, have traveled to India to learn of the special discoveries of some seedy guru about the secrets of life. It is amazing that so many will seek such crumbs which fall from the table of a pagan religious philosopher when the very words of Jesus Christ are available to them to read from the pages of Holy Scripture.

The witchcraft cults in America prosper because of leaders who claim to have discovered the "secret" of prosperity, health, victory over our environment, or some other needed capability. People willingly flock into the train of the religious leader who has "discovered the secret" and is willing to pass it on to them.

Dag Thorleifsson of Iceland has a new cult going. His followers are encouraged to worship the old Viking gods. Another cult is born as a propagandist announces that he has discovered old and long-hidden secrets which he is now willing to make available.

The scientologists, who claim 75,000 followers in the city of Los Angeles alone have "discovered" that man has occupied a number of different bodies during his many incarnations in the world. They profess to be able to prove this by carrying an individual back along a "time track" to his earlier lifetimes to seek out the cause of his current problems.

The claim to special discoveries and "repeatable-on-demand" revelations from God is the point where the cults tend to move off into the occult. Witchcraft, spiritism, and Satan worship are nothing more than religions which claim to be able to call for the incursion of the metaphysical in the realm of the physical. This is surely one of the reasons why the cults are often but a stopping place where a disturbed soul lingers briefly before dropping totally into the pit of the occult.

Nevertheless, the almost universal base of each cult religion is the purported revelation that one person received. These persons claimed divine authority for a private, unauthenticated religious event. They claim to have seen a vision of a woman on a mountain, heard a voice in a prayer tower, or been visited by an angel who came with golden tablets and giant spectacles. The unsubstantiated and largely preposterous stories are endless.

What is the proper response to the claim of an individual to a new, divine discovery? His claim should be subjected to the biblical *rules of evidence*, as we will explain shortly. The discovery may have been an hallucination, an outright lie, or even the result of indigestion or a sleepless night. We cannot know. We are without corroborative evidence.

How different is the truth of Christianity! It is not dependent upon claims by private individuals to special discoveries. The fundamental characteristic of the faith of Christ is that it is based on *historical* fact.

Talking of all of the events that centered around the life, work, death, and resurrection of Christ, the Scripture says, "This thing was not done in a corner" (Acts 26:26). Luke states that Christ declared Himself to be alive after His passion "by many infallible proofs" (Acts 1:3). There were hundreds and in some cases thousands of witnesses to the open and public facts of the Gospel.

Often those to whom the Gospel was preached were reminded that they *knew* of their own knowledge the truth of these things (Acts 26:25-26). The witnesses to the facts of the Gospel were declared as being alive and responsible to testify of Christ (1 Cor. 15:6). Nothing is more obvious in the writings of the Old and New Testaments than the fact of the public revelation and working of God in the presence of proofs and competent witnesses. The truth of Christianity does not depend on private knowledge or secret, unconfirmable relationships on the part of individuals.

But the growing activity of religious promoters with concocted stories should not come as a surprise to us. The Scripture predicts, "There shall be false teachers among you, who privily shall bring in damnable heresies, even denying the Lord that brought them, and bring upon themselves swift destruction. And many shall follow their pernicious ways; by reason of whom the way of truth shall be evil spoken of. And through covetousness shall they *with feigned words* make merchandise of you; whose judgment now of a long time lingereth not, and their damnation slumbereth not" (2 Peter 2:1-3).

We notice that the heresies being brought in by false teachers are *secret* and *destructive*. It would never be possible for these purveyors of their own imaginings to be successful were it not for the foolish inattention on the part of many to the laws of evidence. Jesus Christ paid very careful attention to these laws, saying, "If I bear witness of Myself, My witness is not true" (John 5:31).

Again and again Jesus paid respect to the divine laws of evidence by naming those other sources of data that would bear witness to the truth of His Word. "Jesus answered them, 'I told you, and ye believed not; the works that I do in My Father's name, they bear witness of Me" (John 10:25).

Because of these abundant sources of evidence the Apostle Peter was able to say, "For we have not followed cunningly devised fables, when we made known unto you the power and coming of our Lord Jesus Christ, but were eyewitnesses of His majesty" (2 Peter 1:16).

Nevertheless, the deceitful infection of the cultic promoters continues as they beguile unstable souls away from the clear and obvious truth into unprovable mysteries that they themselves cannot explain.

The Christian who would be a good servant of Jesus Christ in our time does well to take the opposite course. The Prophet Habakkuk gave us good advice in this regard, saying, "And the Lord answered me, and said, 'Write the vision, and make it plain upon tables, that he may run that readeth it' " (Hab. 2:2). The Apostle Paul operated in similar fashion, saying, "We use great plainness of speech" (2 Cor. 3:12).

It is a fair generalization to say that it is the duty of the true minister of the Gospel to take the mysteries of God and make them plain. The normal direction of the cultic promoter is to take the plain truth of the Word and turn it into as mysterious a message as possible. Many deadly pitfalls lie along the path of the dark and the mysterious.

No Christian is required to believe that Jesus Christ has appeared to anyone since the day of the completion of Holy Scripture. God rests His case on the Bible. This Book should be plainly preached by those who stand in pulpits. It should be clearly taught by those who would expound truth. It should be carefully read by all who would discover the nature of reality. Then there will be no need for special discoveries on the part of anyone. The greatest discovery an individual can make is to experience the joy of a personal relationship with Jesus Christ, which comes by faith in His person and His work as revealed in Holy Scripture.

The secret is out! The Gospel is available to all. Jesus Christ has come in the flesh and brought life and immortality to light through the Gospel. Faith in Him brings a discovery that is special indeed and available to all.

8 | Defective Christology

Who is Jesus Christ?

This is the most important question that any person will ever face. The deepest joys we will ever know in this life and our very hope of eternal life depend on the proper answer to that question. Because this is true, we may be sure that the primary activity of Satan will be to obscure as much as possible the true nature of the person of our blessed Saviour, the Lord Jesus.

In all of the history of the Church, the most grievous heresies have been those which have advocated a view of the person of Christ other than that which is taught in the Word of God. Satan knows that an improper understanding of the person and the work of Christ makes salvation impossible.

The attack on the understanding of the nature of

Christ began in the days of the Early Church. The intellectually disposed Colossians began to be infected by a heretical view called Gnosticism. This doctrinal error taught that a human approached the Godhead through progressive steps of higher and higher angelic beings who bridged the gap between man and God. It taught that Christ was one of these angelic beings who was more than man but less than God. It advocated the worship of these angelic beings and included worshiping Christ as merely a part of the duty of a Christian.

The Apostle Paul, knowing the peril the Colossians were in of turning to a religion other than the faith of Jesus Christ, wrote them a most earnest epistle. He warned, "Beware lest any man spoil you through philosophy and vain deceit, after the tradition of men, after the rudiments of the world, and not after Christ. For in Him dwelleth all the fulness of the Godhead bodily" (Col. 2:8-9).

He expanded that warning into the details of their false religion by saying, "Let no man beguile you of your reward in a voluntary humility and worshiping of angels, intruding into those things which he hath not seen, vainly puffed up by his fleshly mind, and not holding the Head" (Col. 2:18-19).

These people prided themself in possessing knowledge. Paul told them that knowledge was *not enough;* they must have "full knowledge" *(epignosis)*. He insisted that this full knowledge was the knowledge of the person of Jesus Christ Himself. The Scripture therefore insists that in worshiping Jesus Christ, we are worshiping God Himself. "He that honoreth not the Son honoreth not the Father" (John 5:23).

Later in the history of the Church there grew up another sub-Christian point of view called Arianism. This was one of the first heresies of the Church, and it was declared so because it denied the true deity of our Saviour, the Lord Jesus Christ.

The advocacy of Arianism by the satanic opponents of Christianity produced great doctrinal clarity in the ranks of the early Christians. These confrontations led them to the greatly reinforced conviction that one's attitude toward the nature of Jesus Christ is primary to his Christianity. A false view of the Saviour produced a false religion which presented no salvation at all. This conviction led the Early Church fathers to earnestly contend for the faith. They knew what was at stake. The issue was the survival of Christianity itself.

So much historical precedent of cultic attacks on the person of Christ should lead us not to be surprised at the cultic detractions today. Most of the cults that are active in our time deny the true deity of Christ, the true humanity of Jesus, or the true union of the two natures in one Person.

Notice the confusing Christian Science view of our Lord Jesus:

> "Jesus is the human man who demonstrated Christ.
> "Christ is the ideal Truth, divine idea, the spiritual or true idea of God.
> "Mary's conception of him was spiritual.
> "Jesus was the offspring of Mary's self-conscious communion with God.
> "At the ascension the human, material concept, or Jesus, disappeared, while the spiritual self, or Christ, continues to exist in the eternal order of divine Science, taking away the sins of the world,

as the Christ has always done, even before the human Jesus was incarnate to mortal eyes.

"His resurrection was not bodily! He reappeared to his students, that is, to their apprehension he rose from the grave—on the third day of his ascending thought!" (*Science and Health*, 1916, 473:15; 332:19; 347:14-15; 332:26-27; 29:32-30:1; 334:10-20; 509:4-7)

The Jehovah's Witnesses are just as confused. They say:

"Jesus Christ, a created individual, is the second greatest Personage of the universe, the first and only direct creation by his Father, Jehovah . . . appointed as His vindicator and the Chief Agent of life toward mankind.

"Born as a human son of God, October, 2 B.C.

"Became the Messiah Seed in Fall, A.D. 29.

"Died on Stake as Ransomer in Spring, A.D. 33.

"Resurrected Immortal on Third Day . . . He was raised 'as a mighty immortal spirit Son' . . . a glorious spirit creature.

"We know nothing about what became of (his body), except that it did not decay or corrupt" (*Make Sure of All Things,*) 1957, p. 207. *Let God Be True*, 1952, pp. 207-210. *Studies in the Scriptures,* II, p. 129).

The Mormons say:

"Jesus Christ is Jehovah, the first-born among the spirit children of Elohim, to whom all others are juniors.

"He is unique in that he is the offspring of a mortal mother and of an immortal, or resurrected and glorified, Father.

"He was the executive of the Father, Elohim, in the work of creation.

"He is greater than the Holy Spirit, which is subject unto him, but His Father is greater than He" (*The Articles of Faith*, Talmage, pp. 471-472. *Doctrine and Covenants* 76:24. *Doctrines of Salvation*, Joseph F. Smith, I, p. 18).

The cultic views of modern liberal theology are little better:

"An idyllic figure.

"The flower of humanity.

"The world's greatest ethical teacher.

"A man so good his deluded followers took him for a god.

"Jesus was divine—and in the same sense, all are divine. The spark of divinity only needs to be fanned into flame.

"In Christ, humanity was divinity and divinity was humanity.

"The recorded miracles of Christ are merely legendary exaggerations of events that are entirely explicable from natural causes.

"Jesus spoke in accommodation with the ideas of His contemporaries and held the current Jewish notions.

"Those who recorded the virgin birth were doubtless influenced by pagan fables, thinking thus to secure for Him the honor of celestial paternity.

"A virgin birth and literal resurrection are no essential part of Christian faith.

"Christ was a master product of evolution."

The fevered minds of the Theosophy people have produced the following:

"Jesus gave to the world fragments of teaching of value as basis for world religion, as did men like Buddha, Confucius, Pythagoras, etc.

". . . at a certain stage in the career of Jesus, the latter was taken possession of by the great Teacher, the Bodhisattva of eastern tradition" (Hugh Shearman, *Modern Theosophy*, 1952, pp. 201-202).

The central truth of Christianity is therefore related to the question, "What think ye of Christ?" The Christian is commanded to test the spirits of these suspicious alternative messengers.

The doctrinal test of those spirits is very clear. "Beloved, believe not every spirit, but try the spirits whether they are of God; because many false prophets are gone out into the world. Hereby know ye the Spirit of God: every spirit that confesseth that Jesus Christ is come in the flesh is of God; and every spirit that confesseth not that Jesus Christ is come in the flesh is not of God; and this is that spirit of antichrist, whereof ye have heard that it should come; and even now already is it in the world" (1 John 4:1-3).

It is clear then that the test of a true representative of the Gospel has to do with his definition of the person and the work of Jesus Christ. The central doctrine of Christianity is *Christology,* the doctrine of the nature of the person of Jesus Christ.

Christianity affirms the true deity and the true humanity of our blessed Saviour, which deity and humanity is conjoined together in one personality on the basis of the hypostatic union. By this we understand that Jesus Christ was not partly man and partly God on the basis of some percentage or formula. He is *true* humanity. He is *true* deity in human form. The characteristic of biblical faith is that it has a proper understanding of the nature of the person of Christ.

There are those today who claim to be Christians who deny the true deity of Christ. Religious liberalism can be judged as heretical on the basis of its denial of the sure deity of the blessed Son of God. Liberalism is not Christianity, it is a heretical, anti-Christian view, being defective in its view of the deity of Christ.

There are religions that deny the true humanity of the Saviour. Christian Science, as an instance, denies the existence of the physical, claiming that the essential substance of the universe is mind. "All is mind" is the index of Mary Baker Eddyism. If the physical does not exist, then deity did not become true humanity in the person of Christ. This is the doctrine of antichrist, according to Scripture.

The thoughtful Christian will carefully analyze the doctrine of a cult that is being pressed upon him, paying special attention to the Christology of that alternative religious message. The message that in effect declares Christ to be the automaton of the Father and not a real person in Himself is a cult. The message that denies the virgin birth of Christ, holding Him to be merely the natural son of Joseph and Mary, is a cult. An examination of the doctrinal base of any religion in the light of its views on the person and the work of Jesus Christ can be most revealing.

The question, "What think ye of Jesus?" is only answered correctly by the believing Christian. The Christian gladly answers, "Jesus Christ is the only begotten Son of the living God, God incarnate in the form of human flesh. He is the Son of man, the only Saviour of the world, the Author and Finisher of our faith, who, through His death on the cross, provides redemption for all who believe in Him.

He is the One who died for our sins, rose again on the third day, who lives to make intercession for us before His Father and who one day will come in His glorious returning to judge the quick and the dead at His appearing in His kingdom. He is Lord and God, and in Him alone we have life, and life more abundantly."

Closely related to the fatal heresy of defective Christology is a denial of the trinity of the Godhead. The only true God is one God, eternally existent in three persons, Father, Son, and Holy Spirit. Each person of the Godhead is co-equal and co-eternal with the others. This view is not held by the Jehovah's Witnesses, who say:

> "There is no authority in the Word of God for the doctrine of the Trinity of the Godhead.
>
> "The Trinity doctrine is unbiblical in origin.
>
> "Rebellion in Eden called into question Jehovah's position as supreme sovereign. The Scriptures abound with evidence that the primary issue before creation is the vindication of Jehovah's name and Word.
>
> "God is a solitary being from eternity, unrevealed and unknown. No one has existed as His equal to reveal Him.
>
> "Jehovah is the almighty and supreme sovereign of the universe—not omnipresent, but with power extending everywhere" (*Studies in the Scriptures,* V, 54 ff. *Make Sure of All Things,* 1957, pp. 191, 386. President Nathan Knorr, *Religion in the 20th Century,* p. 388. *The Kingdom Is at Hand,* p. 507).

Many cults are blind as to the nature of God and in their theology deny the deity of Jesus Christ or the deity of the Holy Spirit. An improper faith in the only true God makes impossible any real hope of salvation.

These critical doctrinal problems concerning the nature of the Godhead should come to each Christian as a new reminder of the need for Christian scholarship. For too long we have been influenced by foolish leaders who say, "We don't need doctrine; we just need experience!"

In the same vein is the mindless claim, "We don't preach doctrine, we just preach Christ!" Preachers who talk like this need to move up from their spiritual kindergartens and realize the shameful neglect of their own personal scholarship and the consequent neglect of doctrinal preaching to their people. The cults will have a field day in exploiting experience-oriented saints who have no time for the study of Christian doctrine.

9 | Segmented Biblical Attention

There is no book in all the world like the Bible.

The Word of God is the most interesting and inspiring reading available to man. It contains many high points of eloquence, illumination, and insight. It tells of the ministry of prophets, apostles, and other inspired men and women who were servants of God. Varying points of emphasis in the Bible strike responsive notes in the varying personalities of the readers. The inevitable result is that each of us has favorite passages of Scripture, portions of the Word of God that were used to meet particular needs at given times. There is nothing wrong with this.

People of a loving disposition are thrilled with 1 Corinthians 13. Those who are judgmental in character enjoy reading 2 Thessalonians 1 or certain passages in the Revelation. Christians with a historical bent are drawn to the passages of the Old Testament which describe the kings and kingdoms of antiquity.

Those of philosophic bent enjoy the didactic conversations of Christ in the Gospels and the logical discourses of Paul. The activists consider the Great Commission the most relevant verse of Scripture, often feeling that theological discussion as to the nature of faith is a colossal waste of time. One can begin to get off base this way.

There are those also who are interested only in semantics. To them, the study of the Word of God is a perpetual game of anagrams. They are constantly counting verses and letters and attributing to them numerical value. They study the Word of God with a dictionary in one hand and a slide rule in the other.

Semanticists are often frightened by the spiritual gladiators who read the Book of Acts as a story of heroic conquest and feel constrained to go and do likewise.

The Bible is also read by sociologist types. These may forever discuss the religio-economic trends that were established by the density of the population of the city of Jerusalem as influenced by the Christian subculture and populatively aerated by the early persecutions.

These sociological Christians are worried about those who concentrate on Paul's description of this life as being "light affliction, which is but for a moment" that works for us a far more exceeding and eternal weight of glory (2 Cor. 4:17). They accuse such ones as being "so heavenly minded they are no earthly good." They warn that Christianity is more than pie in the sky, and consists essentially in loving one's brother—and showing it.

Those disposed to see in the Bible a delineation of forms of worship range from the most informal Quakers to high church Episcopalians. One's emotional disposition affects his convictions as to the teaching of Scripture. Episcopalians from their high church position cannot tell the difference between the Baptists and the Brethren, and the Pietists believe Episcopalians are simply Catholics who flunked Latin.

Human dispositions, responding to the portions of Scripture to which they have given attention, have made of this amorphous thing called "Christianity" a crazy quilt of groups whose resemblance is obscure indeed.

There are, therefore, enough differences between Christians that, if they were properly exploited, the church could become a hotbed of Christian charity! The admonition to keep the unity of the Spirit in the bond of peace is important in the light of the variety of groups, experiences, and emphases that call themselves Christian.

Many organizationally disposed individuals can hardly forgive the Holy Spirit for manifesting Himself in diversity and not in uniformity. We cannot but believe, however, that the diversity of Christian groups is sometimes a good thing and not without the permission of our heavenly Father. Variation and diversity are not marks of error.

But herein lies a potentially serious problem. The temptation of groups of serious conviction is to move ever further from the central pale of reason that C. S. Lewis calls "mere Christianity." Because of their emphasis, they begin declaring that "love is everything," or "history is all-important." They take some important but not critical emphasis of Scripture and move it to the exalted position of an imperative doctrine. They move their test of fellowship away from the person of Jesus Christ to some lesser point.

Soon, wearing a given kind of clothing, visiting the mother church, or some other distinctive becomes a test of fellowship. Such a group may have started well, but, for want of proper attention to the whole counsel of God, they drift away from vital Christianity into a misplaced emphasis.

It is easy to see how a religious group can move from the true to the false by small steps of defection from the teaching of Holy Scripture. The special emphases of many religious groups have been helpful to Christianity. Too often, however, this special emphasis becomes the critical, all-important point. When a theological eccentricity moves to the very center of the attention of a group of Christians, that group, often without sensing it, becomes eccentric and potentially heretical.

This "outward bound" direction must always be avoided by the biblical Christian. When a group develops a theological or doctrinal interpretation that touches only minimally on the proper biblical emphasis and lives for the most part outside of that circle, it becomes a cult.

By this we mean that, from a starting point of Scripture, it has moved away from the teaching of the Word of God so that its central emphasis has become a set of human philosophies, ideas, or revelations that can no longer be justified by the teaching of the Word of God. Its attention to an interesting portion of Scripture has been carried to the point where it has isolated this passage of the Word of God from the corrective modifications found in other portions of the Word. Its segmented biblical attention has cut it off from the body of divine truth.

Virtually every cult in existence today has followed the unwise course of segmented biblical attention out beyond the pale of reason into the production of a destructive heresy.

We have an illustration of this in the Word of God. It involves an encounter between the Apostle Paul and a group which knew only the baptism of John.

> "And it came to pass, that, while Apollos was at Corinth, Paul having passed through the upper coasts came to Ephesus; and finding certain disciples, he said unto them, 'Have ye received the Holy Ghost since ye believed?' And they said unto him, 'We have not so much as heard whether there be any Holy Ghost.' And he said unto them, 'Unto what then were ye baptized?' And they said, 'Unto John's baptism.' Then said Paul, 'John verily baptized with the baptism of repentance, saying unto the people, that they should believe on Him which should come after him, that is, on Christ Jesus.' When they heard this, they were baptized in the name of the Lord Jesus. And when Paul had laid his hands upon them, the Holy Ghost came on them; and they spake with tongues, and prophesied" (Acts. 19:1-6).

Here is the account of disciples who heard and gladly responded to the inspired preaching of John the Baptist. They embraced with sincerity his doctrine of repentance for the remission of sins, "for the kingdom of heaven is at hand." They therefore became disciples of John the Baptist, and we may well assume that they continued faithfully in their conviction of the truth of the message of this humble forerunner of Jesus Christ.

But herein was their problem. They were so taken with the preaching of John that they neglected his major emphasis: namely, that One was coming after him, whose shoe latchets John was unworthy to loosen, who would guide them into all truth. They therefore missed the opportunity to hear the Word of Christ. They missed the chance to believe in Him and become true Christians, sharing in the gift of the Holy Spirit given to the Church on the day of Pentecost. Their own testimony was that they had not even heard of the Holy Spirit.

These people had not come to the place where they shared the life of God that comes to every person who is made a new creature in Jesus Christ. The Apostle Paul's question to these disciples, "Did you receive the Holy Spirit when you believed?" was a most appropriate way of asking whether they had become true Christians.

Realizing that they were not indeed believers, the Apostle Paul said unto them "that they should believe on Him who should come after him" [after John the Baptist, that is]; they should receive Jesus Christ. The happy conclusion of this story is that they did indeed believe on Jesus Christ, were baptized in His name, and received the gift of the Holy Spirit.

We may rejoice that Paul was given of God the opportunity to bring to these sincere seekers after truth the final revelation of God in Jesus Christ. It is highly probable that they would otherwise have formed a religious group around the preaching of John the Baptist which, however sincere, would have prevented people from hearing the message of salvation by the grace of God made possible through Christ alone. Their sincere attention to a segmented, non-final revelation would have therefore been a most damnable thing. Their religious belief and practice would have been merely a cult rather than real and vital Christianity.

The lesson for all of us is very clear. While we may be fascinated with the words of one of the personalities of Scripture and with the emphasis of a given book of the Bible, we must not fail to pay attention to the message of the entire Word of God.

The Bible declares about itself that *"all Scripture is given by inspiration of God and is profitable for doctrine, for reproof, for correction, for instruction in righteousness that the man of God may be perfect, throughly furnished unto all good works"* (2 Tim. 3:16-17). It is therefore of great importance that the doctrine by which a Christian orients his faith and his life come from *all* Scripture. He must remember that the Bible, both Old and New Testaments, was given by inspiration of the Holy Spirit and is vital in its entirety to his understanding of the faith.

He remembers also that revelation is progressive! God presented truth in a cumulative fashion, moving from the basic theistic concepts of the Old Testament to the final revelation of Himself in Jesus Christ. Christ brought life and immortality to light through the Gospel (2 Tim. 1:10), and His doctrine was explained to us by His apostles who wrote the letters of the New Testament.

We must also never forget that the proper interpretation of the Bible must be based on text, context, and greater context. The biblical interpreter must ask, "What does this verse mean? In what setting is it given to us? How does it relate to the whole Bible?"

The major deficiency of the cults of our time is that they have neglected to base their faith on the Bible as a whole. One group denies the immortality of the soul because of a statement about death in Ecclesiastes 9:5. They ignore the fact that the final light on the subject of immortality was given to us by Jesus Christ. Paul explains that to be absent from the body is to be present with the Lord (see 2 Cor. 5:8).

The Way, a cultic fringe of the Jesus movement, denies the existence of the Trinity because of an undue emphasis on the personality of Jesus. The result of this doctrinal disorientation is that this group seems to settle for a psychological encounter with the personality of Jesus as the basis of salvation.

The transcendental meditation people make the same mistake. They read verses in the Bible which tell us to think and meditate, and the rest they get from an Indian guru. Putting their minds into neutral, they suppose that they can think and meditate on nothing and get some final answers. Some very strange personalities have resulted from religions so transcendental that they never touch the ground of a real world. Meditation in moderation is fine, but there comes a time when we must also go to work.

One editorial writer helpfully analyzed the Children of God as follows:

"The Children's tendency to bend the Bible to fit their own whims smacks of cultism and leads to dangerously blind spots in crucial realms of life. They presumptuously accuse Paul of having been out of God's will whenever he worked at tentmaking. (No one has yet suggested this of Christ, who during His 'silent years' presumably worked as a carpenter for pay.) The Children need to be more honest in their use of Scripture. A greater understanding and appreciation of hermeneutics would help" (*Christianity Today*, Nov. 5, 1971, p. 31).

Some who pretend to be experts on demonism fall into the same error. Knowing of demon influence, they proceed to attribute all forms of aberrative behavior to the presence of demons. The final consequence is that laziness, lust, clock-watching, loud talking and all other irresponsible activities are thought to be the result of demonic influence.

There are others who find a verse in the Bible about God having given to some prophet a vision. They use this as the scriptural base for a notion that all sound religion is therefore conducted on the basis of God revealing Himself in visions and dreams. Such a notion can cause a person to drift away from the Word of God into a spiritual opium den of his own making.

Another leader may greatly encourage Christians by his emphasis on a relaxed and positive mental attitude. While this message may be of value, if taken as ultimate truth, it can cause a naive person finally to deny physical reality. No mental attitude can take away the fact of death or deliver us from the necessity of living in the midst of physical dimensions. A positive mental attitude is good when properly applied. At other times it is mere foolishness.

The mature Christian will make none of these mistakes. He will continue in a daily study of the Word of God and apply the teachings of Scriptures in the place and to the degree in which God intended them to be applied. He knows the danger of wresting the Scripture to his own destruction. He will avoid the dread pitfalls of spiritual lunacy that come from going off the deep end on the basis of any one verse from the Bible.

It is a grave temptation for any group to find a verse in the Bible about holiness, the kingdom, law, grace, works, faith, or something else and use it for a substitute for the whole counsel of God. Even zealous Christians have frequently fallen into the trap of segmented biblical interpretation, thereby creating a cultic influence in their system of doctrine.

Christian maturity will save us from all of this.

10 | Enslaving Organizational Structure

"You belong to me!" While these are not exactly the words of a grand old hymn, this is a song title that nicely represents the point of view of almost every cult leader. Cults actually bring their followers into psychological and spiritual slavery.

A very interesting description of the believer in Jesus Christ is found in our Lord's statement, "The wind bloweth where it listeth, and thou hearest the sound thereof, but canst not tell whence it cometh, and whither it goeth; *so is every one that is born of the Spirit*" (John 3:8). We may well sympathize with the response of Nicodemus, the well organized Jewish religionist, when he said, "How can these things be?" Nicodemus was astonished both with the assertion of Jesus Christ about the necessity of the new birth and with this remarkable statement of Christian freedom.

This same theme—the freedom of the person who has become a believer in Jesus Christ—is echoed in many places through the New Testament. "If the Son therefore shall make you free, ye shall be free indeed" (John 8:36). "Where the Spirit of the Lord is, there is liberty" (2 Cor. 3:17). "Let every man be fully persuaded [what is right about doubtful things] in his own mind" (Rom. 14:5). "Ye are bought with a price; *be not ye the servants of men*" (1 Cor. 7:23).

So important to the writers of Scripture is the preservation of Christian freedom that we are not only advised that we possess it, but we are carefully warned never to lose it. "Stand fast therefore in the liberty wherewith Christ hath made us free, and be not entangled again with the yoke of bondage" (Gal. 5:1). The reason we must work to avoid entanglement in the yoke of bondage is "for, brethren, you have been called unto liberty" (Gal. 5:13).

The consequent emphasis of the New Testament is that Christian leaders who have power or persuasive ability must be careful never to overly control or dominate the faith of others. The Apostle Paul never said that the strong should *control* the weak but rather that the strong should *support* the weak.

No doubt there are and always will be individuals whose physical, mental, or spiritual inferiority make them vulnerable to the dominance of others. The religious leader has a solemn obligation to refuse to take advantage of that vulnerability. He must not use his gifts or talents as the leverage to power. He must avoid like the plague the temptation that will surely come to him to organize followers around himself rather than around Christ.

A further expression of heartfelt concern as to the attitude of leadership comes from the Apostle Peter to the elders of the churches. Few passages are more indicative of the divine concern for the proper pastoral attitude than his earnest words, "Neither as being lords over God's heritage, but being examples to the flock" (1 Peter 5:3).

The Word of God is clear; spiritual leadership is to be the leadership of example. In simplicity and godly sincerity, the leader is to be an imitator of Jesus Christ and pray that his very life will furnish, before his onlooking flock, an illustration of the Christian life for all to see. When the life of a Christian leader illustrates only arrogance, groundless authoritarianism, and human imposition, he is representing another Christ than the One presented in Holy Scripture.

The Apostle John, in his third epistle, may well be presenting a vignette glimpse of a leader whose life was characterized by such dreadful presumption. After calling himself simply a "fellow helper to the truth," John says, "I wrote unto the church: but Diotrephes, who loveth to have the preeminence among them, receiveth us not" (v. 9). Here was a leader who was inclined more toward preeminence than piety. The result is that he became an illustration, mentioned by name in Holy Scripture, of the kind of leadership that Christians can do without.

The promoters of the cults obey no such rules as Scripture lays down for leaders. Indeed, they know that their success is directly dependent upon their ability to trap followers into a permanent entanglement. This association is almost invariably

formed with the bonds of fear. The leader's preaching, teaching, and efforts are dedicated, not to the
production of individual competence and freedom
on the part of his followers, but to create dependence. The leaders of the cults are working to
promote, not liberty, but slavery.

Thus an almost universal characteristic of the
cults is the creation of a monolithic, merciless,
and entangling organizational structure. To them
the purpose of a religious organization is not that
it becomes a living segment of the body of Christ
but a personally exploitable syndicate.

We have evidence of the beginning of such a
tendency in the pages of the New Testament. In the
Book of the Revelation, Christ brought specific
messages to seven New Testament churches. An
examination of these messages to the churches
can give us a new reminder of the divine attitude
toward local religious groups. Many of the compli-
ments and criticisms of the seven churches of Asia
Minor are most applicable to religious organizations in our day.

Of particular note is the message given to the
church at Ephesus. Here was a church that was
commended by the Lord because of its many vir-
tues. They were, however, at the starting point
of spiritual defection. Despite this, they were given
a compliment by the Lord Jesus. "But this thou
hast, that thou hatest the deeds of the Nicolaitans,
which I also hate" (Rev. 2:6). The time of
the Early Church was an era of the beginning of
the "deeds," the activities, of a group that are
described by the name *Nicolaitans*.

This group is mentioned in a further note to the
churches, namely the one that was addressed to the

church at Pergamos. This church had progressed farther along the path of spiritual deterioration and so the mention of the Nicolaitans among this group came in a different form. "So hast thou also them that hold the *doctrine* of the Nicolaitans, which thing I hate" (Rev. 2:15).

Who were the Nicolaitans? What were their deeds and their doctrine? We have only one definite indication as to the nature of this group and that comes to us from the meaning of the word itself. The word *Nicolaitan* comes from two Greek words, *nicao* and *laos* which means victory over or subjugation of the people.

The exaggerated distinction between "clergy" and "laity" had begun in the early stages of Christianity. Some were already thinking it spiritually necessary or practical to subjugate the people of God and become masters over them. The super organizers were already appearing in the days of early Christianity. The program of the subjugation of the people had begun! Already the "laymen" were considered exploitable commodities to be mastered by their religious leaders.

We can well imagine the efficient organizers of the churches at Ephesus and Pergamos conversing. "Well, we obviously cannot trust the ignorant men and women who come to our church from the normal pursuits of life to study the Bible for themselves. It is surely our responsibility to interpret God for their lives. After all, that is the responsibility of our exalted leadership."

Power corrupts! This is not only true in the realm of politics. It is tragically true also in the area of religion.

We can be very sure of the attitude of God

toward this program in that He complimented the church at Ephesus for literally *hating* the deeds of the Nicolaitans, about which He said, "I also hate." The Holy Spirit saw fit to restate this attitude when He talked about the development of the doctrine of the Nicolaitans, saying, "Which thing I hate." The religious ascendancy of a group of spiritual elitists over the mass of the people is a program and a belief that is hated by God. We must not ignore the fact that this attitude on the part of God is twice mentioned in these messages to the churches. The Lord is emphasizing to us that the subjugation of the people is a program despised by God.

We may note also that the Nicolaitan trend was merely a set of deeds in the church at Ephesus. By the time we come to the church at Pergamos, however, what had been deeds has turned into a doctrine. How quickly do people work to give official doctrinal sanction to activities which are merely personal or organizational inventions!

Religious institutions today are filled with whole sets of catechisms, disciplines, liturgies, and stated methods which are basically nothing but the doctrine of the Nicolaitans. Who can doubt but that many religious organizations of our time are efforts to organize people around some central loyalty other than Jesus Christ Himself. This indeed was the criticism that was leveled against the otherwise commendable church at Ephesus. The Lord said, "Nevertheless I have somewhat against thee, because thou hast left thy first love" (Rev. 2:4).

The church at Ephesus was warned that it had fallen and must repent and do its first works or else its candlestick would be removed and its light of testimony extinguished. So it is that the landscape of Western Civilization today is dotted with dark, spectral church buildings, ancient artifacts that are nothing but the crumbled remains of a viable testimony that is no more. The program of subjugation of the people kills the true work of Christ.

This kind of killing organizational structure is one of the reliable indexes of the cults of our time. The cult demands total commitment by its convert to an entangling organization, enmeshing him in an impossible set of human rules. Like a fly, he moves into the web. Soon comes the spider.

Whatever else the cultic leaders may be, they are super-organizers. It is impossible for a cult to succeed without conserving its gains and enrolling its followers with increasingly demanding obligations to the leader and the organization. The cult is usually represented to the captured devotee as synonymous with the kingdom of God itself.

One of the normal connotations of the word "cultic" is that of passionate devotion to a cause to the point of the irrational. The cult hopes to bring its hapless followers to the place where they think of little else except their involvement with the movement and its human leader. The average cultist is as much a slave to his present religious involvement as he ever was to the sin of his former life.

This was precisely the accusation which Christ leveled at the Pharisees. "Ye lade men with burdens grievous to be borne" (Luke 11:46). "While they promise them liberty, they themselves are the servants of corruption; for of whom a man is overcome, of the same is he brought in bondage" (2 Peter 2:19).

The present-day Children of God demand that their youthful followers rob their parents before disappearing into the folds of this cultic Jesus religion. Organizational initiation is followed by peer group pressure until finally the pitiful devotee is terror-stricken at the prospect of dropping out of his suspicious entanglements.

The Armstrong people have repeatedly announced that all others beside the members of the Worldwide Church of God are lost for eternity. The Jehovah's Witnesses claim the same for themselves. In this they are not primarily stating a theological proposition; they are merely exerting pressure for membership in their organizations.

There are large religious groups in the world, some of them thought of as legitimate, which preach the doctrine of damnation for all outside their particular organization.

The Christian has been delivered from all such nonsense. He knows that the word *loyalty* is only applicable in a final sense when applied to our relationship to Jesus Christ Himself. The devotion that Christians have for one another is in loving response to the indwelling Holy Spirit, not submission to an enslaving external organization.

It is a truism that the less truth a movement represents, the more highly it must organize. Truth has its own magnetism producing loyalty. The absence of truth makes necessary the application of the bonds of fear.

A cultic leader may present his wares by saying, "Come to Jesus," but his real theme song is "You belong to me." The Christian is well advised to heed the advice of the Apostle Paul, "Stand fast therefore in the liberty wherewith Christ hath made us free, and be not entangled again with the yoke of bondage" (Gal. 5:1).

The only *imperative* membership which the true Christian recognizes is membership in the body of Christ. While he may well belong to a group which places great emphasis on membership in the local church, being a Christian he places no confidence in this as the *basis for his eternal life.* The perceptive Christian is a unique kind of an individual in that he is unable to be "organized" in the same sense as others who place life-and-death importance on their organizational involvement. Jesus Christ has set him free, and no one is entitled to take this freedom from him.

11 | Financial Exploitation

The marvelous message of the Gospel of Christ is that one may receive eternal salvation "without money and without price."

The New Testament Scriptures tell us that salvation comes to us as an absolutely free gift. "The gift of God is eternal life" (Rom. 6:23). We are "justified freely by His grace" (Rom. 3:24). The word *freely* means *without a cause*.

The grace of Jesus Christ is the all-pervading doctrine that applies both to the reception of salvation and our continued walk with God. By the grace of Jesus Christ, each of us has become rich. "For ye know the grace of our Lord Jesus Christ, that, though He was rich, yet for your sakes He became poor, that ye through His poverty might be rich" (2 Cor. 8:9).

The Christian is rich indeed! He has received

the wonderful gift of justification by faith and a thousand derivative benefits. All of this comes to him because of the expenditure of the blood of Jesus Christ on Calvary's cross. He is what he is by the grace of God.

It is clear also from the Word of God that the Christian is never put under obligation to do, give, sacrifice, or expend himself in any way in order to be more sure that he has the gift of God which is eternal life. He is invited in many earnest ways to commit himself to the service of Christ and to become a useful instrument in the hands of God. The Word of God, however, is clear that service for Christ is a voluntary proposition on the part of the Christian, and nothing that he does will increase his own guarantee of eternal life. He is saved by grace and kept by the power of God. His eternal life came to him without payment on his part. It is dependent wholly on the work of Christ on the cross.

It is also clear in Scripture that the gifts, the power, the blessing of God in the life of a Christian do not come because of his ability to purchase them with money, because of his giving to God. We have a fascinating vignette in the Book of Acts. It seems that a man called Simon, who was previously involved in sorcery, became a believer in Jesus Christ. He saw the remarkable power of the apostles through the wonderful working of the Holy Spirit, and he immediately saw the possibilities in the use of such power.

> "And when Simon saw that through laying on of the apostles' hands the Holy Ghost was given, he offered them money, saying, 'Give me also this power, that on whomsoever I lay hands, he may receive the Holy Ghost.' But Peter said unto

him, 'Thy money perish with thee, because thou hast thought that the gift of God may be purchased with money. Thou hast neither part nor lot in this matter; for thy heart is not right in the sight of God. Repent therefore of this thy wickedness, and pray God, if perhaps the thought of thine heart may be forgiven thee' " (Acts 8:18-22).

Quite obviously here, the gifts and the power of God were not a purchasable commodity. Special blessing was hardly available to this man because of his financial offer. Indeed the opposite was true. Peter said to him, "For I perceive that thou art in the gall of bitterness, and in the bond of iniquity" (Acts 8:23). We have no teaching in the New Testament whatsoever that one develops an inside track with God or a greater certainty of salvation because of his giving.

There is another lesson that is very clear from this story. The true leaders of the Church were utterly offended at the suggestion that their favor or the favor of their God could be gained with money. They accused the one who made this offer of terrible sin and said that he was surely under the judgment of God.

We may thank the Lord that the apostles were really members of the untouchables; they were incorruptible people whose fidelity to Jesus Christ was beyond the power of money to buy. Indeed, in their ministries they spoke against the power of money again and again, saying finally. "The love of money is the root of all evil" (1 Tim. 6:10). They invited Christians to give gladly out of a full heart, but they conducted their own lives on a plane of personal sacrifice. And they maintained utter rectitude as to the reception and the use of money.

They even went further than this. They taught that sacrificial Christian leaders thereby gave evidence of their faithfulness to Jesus Christ. By contrast they said that a characteristic of false teachers was that they were those "supposing that gain is godliness" (1 Tim. 6:5). Peter, when speaking of false teachers, said, "And through covetousness shall they with feigned words make merchandise of you" (2 Peter 2:3).

The Apostle Paul, again leaving us a shining example, was very careful never to accept gifts from the churches for his own personal use. He said, "These hands have ministered unto my necessities, and to them that were with me" (Acts 20:34). He did this for the purpose of making the Gospel of Jesus Christ totally without charge. The Church of Christ is the richer because of the peerless standard of personal sacrifice that was left for us by the apostles of Christ.

Happy is the Christian leader who at the end of his life can say with Paul, "I have coveted no man's silver, or gold, or apparel. Yea, ye yourselves know, that these hands have ministered unto my necessities, and to them that were with me. I have showed you all things, how that so laboring ye ought to support the weak, and to remember the words of the Lord Jesus, how He said, 'It is more blessed to give than to receive'" (Acts 20:33-35). The Apostle Paul both preached and practiced the proposition that the love of money is the root of all evil.

What a contrast we see in the cultic practitioner of today! He strongly implies that money contributed to the cause will buy privileges or gifts or powers for the receptive follower. He offers healing for $100. He offers deliverance from accident for life for $1,000. The follower of the cult is often promised that he can escape the many purgatories in this world and the next through the investment of his money.

In the financial structure of the average cult, tithing is but the beginning. Then comes the real pressure. The follower, as the screw is turned, is exploited to the point of economic exhaustion. The stories are legion of wives and children who have been brought to the point of hunger and impoverishment because of the cultic contributions of the head of the family. Enamored of his new spiritual leader, the head of the house forgets the clear teaching of Scripture, "If any provide not for his own, and specially for those of his own house, he hath denied the faith, and is worse than an infidel" (1 Tim. 5:8).

The consequence is that conscienceless religious leaders have provided for themselves massive homes, spacious estates, and large holdings in the commercial world. Some of them even quote as their excuse, "No good thing will He [God] withhold from them that walk uprightly" (Ps. 84:11). What is this but wresting the Scripture to one's own destruction?

The newspapers have carried many stories of shameless financial exploitation by cult leaders. Guru Maharaj Ji, arguing that he should be treated like a god, encourages lavish financial gifts to be given to him and to his family. Armstrong presses his followers to triple-tithe for the support of his cult. How else could private jets be purchased and operated for his personal use in the keeping up of his image?

It is fair to say that an almost universal characteristic of the cults is an insatiable financial appetite in the leadership. They cruelly dangle their followers over the fires of hell as the punishment for not giving large amounts of money to their cause.

The false religions of the world are characterized by lavish temples, overlaid with gold and studded with diamonds. Most of them stand in the midst of a sea of poverty which the cults themselves have caused. Their apparent prosperity is nothing more than the shameful result of their cruel exploitation of frightened people who seek their favors with financial gifts.

The illustrations could go on and on; they are endless. We dare to pray that true Christianity will become increasingly an illustration of the opposite point of view, the free grace of Jesus Christ.

We may rejoice in the vast sums of money that have been given by earnest Christians over the years. The result is that local churches, missionary efforts, radio broadcasts, literature ministries, and hundreds of other solid spiritual endeavors have flourished as sincere Christians have poured out of their gifts and their earnest prayers. Let us pray, however, that there shall not be, within the ranks of true Christianity, those who presume on the saints, thinking of people as sources of economic capability rather than eternal souls.

12 | Denunciation of Others

When one announces himself as the true Messiah, all others of course are false and must be put down. Some of the most bitter imprecations in print are the scathing calumny of cultic messiahs upon all who do not believe their views and join their organizations.

One sometimes suspects that these leaders are infected with a horrible inferiority complex, pushing them to a neurotic defensiveness. They are for the most part unwilling to appear in public debate or answer questions from perceptive Christian scholars concerning the nature of their faith. Expressing their persecution complex, they denounce all alternative views as being satanic and corrupt.

The contrast of true Christianity is very marked. The Bible teaches that there is one Saviour, Jesus Christ, and one way of salvation, faith in His finished work on the cross. Within that wonderful circle of faith once delivered to the saints, however, the Scripture allows for a great diversity of views. Each individual Christian is a believer-priest, and he is related to God as a person.

The Apostle Paul, in writing to the Philippians on the subject of Christian unity, said, "Let us therefore, as many as be perfect, be thus minded; and if in any thing ye be otherwise minded, God shall reveal even this unto you" (Phil. 3:15). In writing to Timothy, he suggested that his views be considered against the final light of divine understanding. He sharply disagreed with Barnabas over John Mark on one of his missionary journeys (Acts 15:38-39), but this same John Mark was later used of the Holy Spirit to write the Gospel of Mark and was acknowledged by Paul as a useful Christian worker (2 Tim. 4:11).

Peter claimed that some of Paul's writings were "hard to be understood" (2 Peter 3:16), but recognized Paul as a beloved brother who was writing according to the wisdom that was given unto him.

Christ prayed for the very people crucifying Him, saying, "Father, forgive them, for they know not what they do."

Paul recognized that some rejected him, but he prayed that it would not be laid to their account. "At my first answer no man stood with me, but all men forsook me; I pray God that it may not be laid to their charge" (2 Tim. 4:16).

True Christians are forbidden to judge one another (Rom. 14:13) and are given the liberty to be persuaded in their own minds as to how to live unto the Lord (Rom. 14:5). They are even told to "judge nothing before its time" (1 Cor. 4:5).

The cultic attitude is a fearful contrast. Herbert Armstrong says:

> "There is only one work that is preaching the true gospel of the kingdom of God—the rule and the reign of God—to the nations. This is that work. Then those who have their part in this work and are converted must constitute the Church of God!
>
> "Every other work rejects the message of Jesus Christ or else rejects His rule through His laws. There is no exception.
>
> "Yes, this work is the work of the true church of God. All others are satanic counterfeits! It is time we come out from among them and become separate."

The Jehovah's Witnesses have also distributed millions of leaflets announcing:

> "God will destroy all false religion soon.
>
> "God has given the world's religions a long time to prove what they are. Today we see their rotten fruitage all over the earth.
>
> "The Bible shows that God's day for accounting is now at hand. For the honor of His own name, which has long been slandered, and for the eternal good of all persons who love righteousness, God must and will act. What will He do?
>
> "His inspired Word compares the world empire of false religion to a grossly immoral woman named 'Babylon the Great.' She is 'richly adorned,' living in 'shameless luxury.' In her is found the 'blood of all earth's slaughtered.' God sentences her to be 'burned with fire,' completely destroyed. (See Revelation chapters 17 and 18.) This destruction will come from the very political powers

that she has dominated for so long. What does this mean for you?" (*"Has Religion Betrayed God and Man?"*)

By this they mean that all other religious points of view except that of the Jehovah's Witnesses are condemned.

The sincere Christian will conduct himself very carefully when it comes to criticism of others. The often repeated sense of Scripture is that the work of God is carried on by many individuals, no one of whom can claim that he has a corner on the market so far as divine revelation is concerned. Christ told His disciples, "Other men labored, and ye are entered into their labors" (John 4:38).

We are therefore reminded in Scripture that one is guilty of the most forbidden kind of arrogance when he presumes to judge the activity of his brothers who labor for the Lord. "Who art thou that judgest?" (Rom. 14:4) "Why dost thou judge thy brother?" (Rom. 14:10) True laborers for Christ are admonished to "keep the unity of the Spirit in the bond of peace" (Eph. 4:3). Paul also writes, "Let us therefore follow after the things which make for peace, and things wherewith one may edify another" (Rom. 14:19).

We are often warned in Scripture to be very suspicious of those whose first calling seems to be to produce divisions within the Church of Christ. When grievous wolves from the outside enter in, or when from the ranks of Christians there are those who arise "speaking perverse things" (Acts 20:30), there are bound to be those who turn their attention from the things of the Lord to a new fascination with the provocative words of an aspiring human leader.

Much unsettlement has been caused in the ranks of Christians by those with pretended convictions who demand a hearing and who are often purveyors of a new discovery of truth. Therefore the Apostle Paul earnestly exhorted, "Now I beseech you, brethren, mark them which cause divisions and offences contrary to the doctrine which ye have learned; and avoid them. For they that are such serve not our Lord Jesus Christ, but their own belly; and by good words and fair speeches deceive the hearts of the simple" (Rom. 16:17-18).

13 | Syncretism

We must become all things to all men!

This worthy goal, reflecting a statement of principle by the Apostle Paul (1 Cor. 9:22), ought to be adopted by every Christian. The witness for Christ must find a way to establish contact with people who come from different cultural, religious, and racial backgrounds. The first problem of anyone who would reach others for Christ is to find a way to minister the eternal truth of the Word of God in language that can move across walls of culture and prejudice. The Christian communicator must find appropriate ways to "become as" the people to whom he ministers.

Within this total context, however, is a line beyond which we must not move. The loving concern for spiritual accommodation can be pressed to the point where it compromises the Gospel of

Christ, sometimes beyond recognition. This kind of accommodation involves one in a grievous sin called syncretism.

Syncretism describes the attempt to gather together what some would call "the best qualities" of various religious points of view into a new and acceptable faith. It is the attempt to "synchronize" the otherwise diverse religious elements currently believed by people so as to make a new religion attractive. The definition of syncretism from a religious point of view is "the process of growth through coalescence of different forms of faith and worship or through accretions of tenets, rights, etc., from those religions which are being superseded" (Webster).

Syncretism is a favorite cultic device. Both the older and the emergent cults, almost without exception, have accommodated themselves to existing religious points of view, incorporating older doctrines into their systems of faith along with new and creative heresies. Few cults of our time present much that is really new in the world of religion. Almost invariably they are a rehash of existing concepts, orthodox and heretical. They present warmedever elements of Protestantism, Catholicism, paganism, pantheism, idolatry, local fetishes, and some pure idiocy.

One can almost imagine a cult promoter looking at a city or a country and asking himself, "What will these people buy? What are their hopes, dreams, prejudices, hang-ups, and how can I give them a religious view that they will support?" The cult promoter is not so foolish as to come on the scene talking initially about the Great Pumpkin, or green men form Mars. He talks about Christ, the Bible, the Holy Spirit, miracles, and other elements of the Christian revelation. The untutored listener is impressed, often believing this person to be a Christian who is just a little wiser than most.

Then comes the hooker. The cult organizer subtly introduces his theological non sequitur. He may, like the Process Church, suggest that Lucifer is not really an enemy of God, but one of His better friends. He may, like Mary Baker Eddy, suggest that personal benefit comes not from the gracious hand of God but from the proper state of mind. It happens in a hundred ways and in a thousand places as the wolf in sheep's clothing presents his "composite religious views" to deceive the unwary.

It happens in our major cities. Los Angeles, for instance, is the great boiling pot of new religions. Its sacred temples, golden altars, religious sciences, midnight séances, healing potions, miraculous handkerchiefs, pyramid power, and "the spiritual gospel of relativity" all testify to the spiritual vulnerability of this and other metropolitan areas.

Sensing some new, exploitative possibilities, the cultist glues together a bewildering array of religious components, knowing that some of these will strike a chord of response. He reaches into every conceivable human interest, promising the benefits of transcendental meditation, psycho-cybernetics, spiritual rationalization, and mental science. Incorporating these in the same package with a few theological terms, he is off and running with another cult.

A similar thing also happens on the mission fields of the world. Missionaries, some of them with merely para-Christian backgrounds, arrive in an area already steeped in religion. Animism, ancestor worship, religious paganism, or raw heathenism are flourishing. Hoping to minimize the offense of their "Christianity," the missionaries accommodate themselves to the local religious climate. Sometimes the resulting religion brings together a regional god, an animal sacrifice, the Virgin Mary, and Jesus Christ all in the same system. Syncretism on mission fields is becoming one of the scandals of the religious world. A syncretistic religion is not Christianity at all; it is a cult.

The cults have been syncretists for a long time. Mary Baker Eddy is an illustration of this. She was impressed with a certain faith healer, P. P. Quimby, a semi-spiritualist. Her imagination was triggered as to ways of merging his views with the Bible. Quimby himself started with old-fashioned mesmerism and soon developed his own version of this mental healing gimmick.

The Worldwide Church of God is also an illustration of syncretism. The Armstrong people picked up a few ideas from the Seventh Day Adventists and tied them with British Israelism. These, with a few extra ideas about diet, health, and the messianic leadership of Armstrong, produced a new and attractive religious combination. This plus religious promotion produced a religion which now takes in a million dollars a week in America.

Evangelical Christians look with understandable astonishment at such syncretistic cults. We do well to remember, however, that syncretism can be a very subtle, creeping heresy, moving into many unexpected places. We hear talk in churches today that may open the door to acceptance of a religious potpourri that is something other than Christianity.

A Christian theologian was heard to say at a recent conference that the great need in the world today is for the message of Christianity to become "a full-orbed Gospel for the whole man." Eloquent sentences such as this sound beautiful, but they can become the open door to many a grievous heresy. When anybody's gospel becomes more "full-orbed" than the Gospel which is very carefully stated in the Word of God, that full-orbed gospel ceases to be the Gospel at all.

What is the Gospel? The Gospel is the good news of salvation in Christ which is very categorically defined in the Word of God. When writing to the Corinthian church, which was already infected with heresy, the Apostle Paul said,

> "Moreover, brethren, I declare unto you the Gospel which I preached unto you, which also ye have received, and wherein ye stand; by which also ye are saved, if ye keep in memory what I preached unto you, unless ye have believed in vain. For I delivered unto you first of all that which I also received, how that Christ died for our sins according to the Scriptures; and that He was buried, and that He rose again the third day according to the Scriptures" (1 Cor. 15:1-4).

It is clear from this definition of the Gospel that there is no "full-orbed gospel for the whole man." That is, the Gospel does not of itself promise to change the social structure, the political climate, or the physical environment of those who, even after exercising faith in Christ, live in the midst of a fallen world. When the Gospel gets wider, more inclusive than Paul's definition in this passage, it ceases to be the Gospel and becomes merely a set of unattainable religious promises.

There are still other forms of subtle syncretism. Many groups of Christians today rejoice in the Gospel plus a wonderful religious heritage. The sacred traditions of many religious groups have been a significant source of stability as they guide their way through the new problems of this current generation. "Our fathers" have bequeathed to many of us a sacred trust in the teachings of Scripture which has stood us in good stead during our moments of spiritual vertigo.

Looking to the past, however, can produce subtle deceptions in our Christian thinking. Surely what the Church needs today is not so much the "faith of our fathers," but the faith of Jesus Christ as expressed in the changeless Scriptures of the New Testament. Heritage can become a dangerous element in the thinking of Christians because it is almost always applied to a human tradition which, at best, is only partially bibical. Indeed, great, time-spanning religious traditions are ordinarily formed to protect by custom certain theological propositions which are unvoiced in the Word of God. "Our sacred heritage" is more often than not a melodramatic expression used to call for loyalty to someone else beside Jesus Christ and something else beside the truth of Scripture.

Another syncretistic tendency has been the movement of the great denominations to include "the imperative of social action" in their preaching of the Gospel. This has been true to the extent that they have been legitimately accused of preaching a social gospel.

Now many evangelical Christians are speaking about "the social implications of the Gospel in our time." Soon the word *implications* changes to the word *responsibilities*. It is but a short step to move from here to the use of the word *imperatives*.

When asked, "What are the social implications of the Gospel?" many an earnest evangelical begins to speak swelling words of wisdom which are simply impossible to understand. Many sound as if they had learned their theology in a sociology class at a third-rate university and have yet to put $10 under their indigent neighbor's sugar bowl in the name of Jesus Christ.

The Gospel may indeed have social implications (fewer, I think, than are commonly touted), but this is another, infinitely less important subject than the death of Jesus Christ on the cross and His glorious resurrection. The one produces eternal salvation; the other, endless discussion.

The point is that Christians need an understanding of Christian doctrine adequate to discern the difference between what the Gospel *is* and what the Gospel implies. We need to comprehend anew that which is absolute about the revelation of Jesus Christ and those things which are relative in decreasing steps of importance.

Political change, physical healing, peace marching, temperance activities, clothing styles—the list is endless—are all interesting subjects for Christian discussion. They are not however to be put in the same class with the finished work of Jesus Christ on the cross by which He takes away the sins of the world.

Christianity has had a very interesting past. We may talk about the Church of Christ moving "like a mighty army" from its early beginnings in the city of Jerusalem to the place where it has swept across the far reaches of Western Civilization. The fact of the matter is that it has not been quite like that. A high percentage of the countries that have been moved by the Gospel of Jesus Christ in other times are now custodians of a dead religion that still masquerades under the name "Christianity." The horizon of practically every city in Western Civilization is dotted with the steeples of buildings called churches which are but grim, spectral monuments of a past life that is now gone.

Europe resembles a vast cemetery of the Christian religion; it is now dead but has left behind its grave markers. Little of Christianity remains in the countries of its origin.

The record seems to show that our faith has prospered best in new and pioneer situations on the cutting edge of civilization as it moved from East to West. As churches grew older, they seem to have given themselves to the spirit of accommodation while forgetting their heavenly calling. They set up ecumenical movements, national conferences of Christians and Jews, and endless other movements to make their situation more legitimate. They opted for political change, social action, and worked with sincerity to redress the grievances of the oppressed within society. Time, money and irreplaceable human energy went into these "worthy causes" and salvation from sin seemed pale by comparsion.

What was the consequence? In country after country the Gospel of Jesus Christ was forgotten. Churches died and never knew it! The glory and the blessing of God departed, and preoccupied religionists were too blind to sense that their candlestick had been removed.

Syncretism, the attempt to synchronize the Gospel of Christ with a godless world, is a deadly

virus from which almost no institution recovers.
This virus can infect us all and, becoming a plague,
can carry us all away. When the Son of man is come,
will He find the faith on the earth?

14 | What Shall We Do?

It is surely the case that we are today seeing a spawning of satanic cults in a measure almost beyond comprehension. Some of the old cults are splitting into several new varieties, and new cults are beginning with every week that passes. Clever individuals with a smattering of religious knowledge are emboldened by their own pride and motivated by Satan to press for their own piece of influence in today's religious scene.

In the face of all of this, concerned people are asking as never before what they can do to protect themselves and their loved ones from these terrible subversive religious influences. Surely the course of action that we who would be true to Christ must take includes the following activities and directions of study:

1. *Understand Christian doctrine.* The chief

single reason for the success of the cults is the spiritual naiveté on the part of many. Too many Christians are content with a superficial knowledge of the Word of God and think of themselves as thereby being spiritually intelligent. Nothing could be farther from the truth!

The Christian must give himself to a detailed study of Scripture and must understand the Bible from a doctrinal point of view. He should have valid biblical information that answers the questions: Who is God? What is man? What is sin? What do we mean by biblical inspiration? Many other questions are imperative points of understanding in the Christian life.

We live in a time when doctrine has been played down in favor of Christian experience. This is the most foolish course imaginable because experience has little or nothing to do with Christian truth. Our experiences are merely human. They are the responses of our nervous system to spiritual truth or error that impinges on our minds and hearts.

The evangelical leader who says, "We do not need more doctrine, but more experience" should rethink his statement. He is playing into the hands of the cultic wolves who prowl on the edges of the flock. The simple lambs who pursue additional feelings may get their titilation from the big, bad, but friendly wolf.

2. *Separation from spiritual subversion.* The Apostle Paul carefully warned the Ephesians, "Have no fellowship with the unfruitful works of darkness" (Eph. 5:11). Many people ask whether they should not attend meetings of cultic religious organizations and give themselves to an extensive reading of subversive religious literature. With

rare exceptions, the answer to this question is no, a thousand times no!

An inquiry into the nuances of false doctrine is an endless pursuit indeed. Few people have the time or the available energy to know all that can be known about the myriad of false religious philosophies of our time. It is not true that we cannot speak critically of false doctrine unless we have read everything that the leadership of these cults has to say. One only has to eat a good steak to realize that the contents of a thousand garbage cans are simply beneath his standards.

There are foolish Christians who are too inquisitive and who ought to heed the advice of Stuart Hamblin's song, "Why should I fool with calico, when I have silk at home?" The statement that says, "You cannot know what it is until you have tried it" is a satanic doctrine, and it is the very one that he used to subvert Eve and bring the terrible cancer of sin into all of the world.

3. *Refuse profane points of view.* These are the very words with which Paul advised Timothy, "Refuse profane and old wives' fables" (1 Tim. 4:7). The Apostle Paul was aware that the world would be filled with spiritual exhibitionists and religious lunatics who would tie up the time and energy of anyone willing to listen to them, doing this for hours and even days.

We live in a time in which stories come to us about pictures of Christ in the clouds, resurrections in remote jungle areas, preachers in some obscure town with a new and unheard of doctrine—the stories are endless.

Christians are enjoined not to give themselves to these things but rather to follow the good advice also extended to Timothy, "Give attendance to reading, to exhortation, to doctrine" (1 Tim. 4:13). Further, we are called upon to "meditate upon these things; give thyself wholly to them, that thy profiting may appear to all" (1 Tim. 4:15).

It is clear then that the Christian must not float through life on the wave of some existential euphoria. Rather the Scripture commands again and again that he must be careful, take heed, watch, remember. He is called upon to be very sober because his satanic adversary continues to go about seeking whom he may devour (1 Peter 5:8).

4. *Do not encourage cultic practitioners.* The Christian is supposed to be loving in his attitude toward people, but he must also face the hard truth that many deceivers have come into the world who do not believe the Gospel of Jesus Christ and are in fact enemies of the Lord. They are antichrist. Concerning these he is admonished to be very careful and not to risk his spiritual stability by allowing himself to be deceived.

The Apostle John wrote: "Whosoever transgresseth, and abideth not in the doctrine of Christ, hath not God. He that abideth in the doctrine of Christ, he hath both the Father and the Son. If there come any unto you, and bring not this doctrine, receive him not into your house, neither bid him God speed; for he that biddeth him God speed is partaker of his evil deeds" (2 John 9-11). This is the hard but the necessary course of action for one who would protect himself and his family from spiritual danger.

5. *Be willing to contend for the faith.* Scripture calls upon us to earnestly contend for the faith, which means of course to be willing to defend the

truth of the Gospel in the face of satanic adversaries (Jude 3). We have illustrations in Scripture that this sometimes means coming to a point of contention with friends and associates. The Apostle Paul was surely a beloved friend of the Apostle Peter, but he said, "When Peter was come to Antioch, I withstood him to the face, because he was to be blamed" (Gal. 2:11). In this case Peter was guilty of doctrinal error and was thereby cooperating with the Judaizers who were subverting the people of Galatia into heresy.

Indeed Jesus Christ Himself had on one occasion to turn to His beloved friend, also the Apostle Peter, and say, "Get thee behind Me, Satan" (Matt. 16:23). The true servant of Jesus Christ must be careful that his friendship with Jesus Christ is the association that is absolute. By comparison to this, all human associations are relative.

The first principle of the universe is truth and this must be defended even at the cost of our lives. Surely the Apostle Paul was serious when he named us all as soldiers of the cross and gave us a detailed list of the armor that we should wear in order to function properly as contenders for the faith (Eph. 6:10-20).

Our spiritual sentiments, and this is the most sentimental age in the history of the Church, would lead us many times to feel that contention for the faith of the Gospel is somehow unspiritual or undignified. Nothing could be farther from the truth. The analogy of the Christian being a soldier of the cross is one that is repeated many times in Holy Scripture. The world is described as a battleground and the essential struggle on that field of conquest is the struggle between truth and untruth.